**Think
Through
History**

Modern Minds

The twentieth-century world

Authors:

Jamie Byrom

Christine Counsell

Michael Gorman

Derek Peaple — from Big Brother

Michael Riley

LONGMAN

Modern Minds – The twentieth-century world

1900   1910   1920   1930   1940   1950

WORLD WAR I 1914–18

WORLD WAR II 1939–45

1914 Arch Duke assassinated at Sarajevo
1916 Battle of the Somme
1917 Russian Revolution
1919 Treaty of Versailles
1921 Partition of Ireland
1924 Death of Lenin

1933 Adolf Hitler became Chancellor of Germany
1939 German troops invaded Poland
1940 Evacuation of British Army from Dunkirk
1941 USA declared war on Japan

The making of minds

1950 1960 1970 1980 1990 2000

1953 Death of Stalin
1962 Cuba missiles crisis
1964 China tested an atomic bomb
1979 Soviet Union invaded Afghanistan
1985 Mikhail Gorbachev came to power in Soviet Union
1989 Berlin Wall came down
1992 Break-up of Soviet Union
1993 Murder of Stephen Lawrence in London
1999 McPherson Report

Two bullets and twenty million deaths

Why did a murder lead to war in 1914?

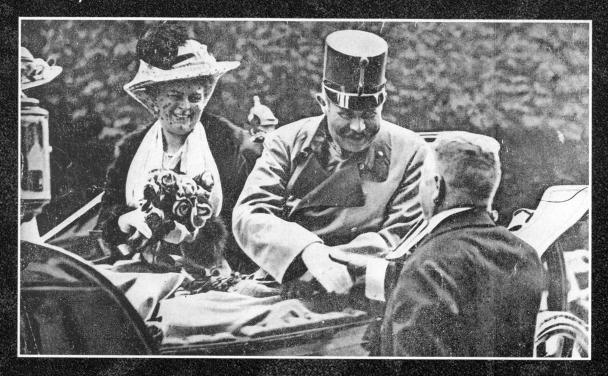

A photograph of Archduke Franz Ferdinand and his wife on the day of their assassination

It was 28 June 1914. The sun shone down on Sarajevo in Bosnia. People on the streets were still talking about the bomb. They were amazed that two such important visitors had dared to visit this very dangerous place. The Archduke Franz Ferdinand and his wife Sophie were either very brave or completely mad. A bomb had been thrown at their car as it passed through the streets. The Archduke had deflected it so that it exploded far enough away to leave him and his wife unharmed. Now they were driving out of the city to safety – or so they hoped.

Their car took a wrong turning. It had to stop and reverse. The driver struggled to change gear. Next to the car on the pavement stood a young man who could not believe his luck. He was one of the terrorists whose bomb attack had failed just minutes before. He was sure that fate was giving him a second chance to destroy his enemy. He took out a pistol and stepped towards the car. He fired two shots. The first hit the Archduke just below the throat and the second struck Sophie in the stomach. They died within minutes. The young assassin had fired his two bullets. He had killed his two victims and – without meaning to – he had also sent twenty million others to their deaths.

Your enquiry

Of course it is impossible for two bullets to kill twenty million people. But the violent death of the Archduke and his wife was to form a vital link in the long chain of events which led to what we now call the First World War. At the end of this enquiry you will make a display about this strange chain of events and show how it led to a war which changed the world.

Nations and empires

If we are to understand the chain of events leading to the First World War, we need to know more about the murder in Sarajevo.

The Archduke Franz Ferdinand was from one of Europe's most powerful royal families. He was the **heir** to the throne of Austria-Hungary. Austria-Hungary was more than a single nation: it was a vast **empire** which spread across central Europe. All these different lands were ruled by the Austrian emperor.

Inside Austria-Hungary there were many different races of people. There were Germans, Czechs, Slovenes, Croats – and there were the Serbs. Gavrilo Princip, the young man who had killed the Archduke and his wife, was a Serb.

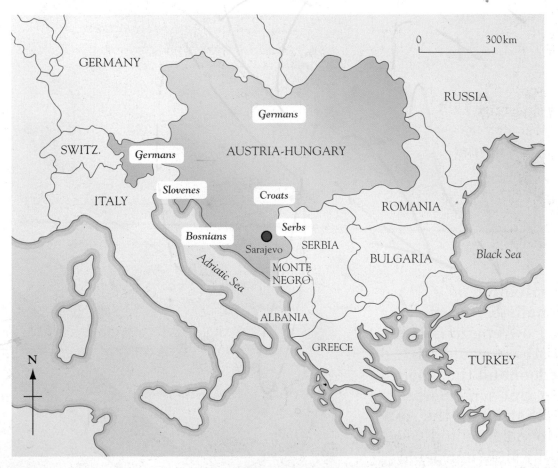

The empire of Austria-Hungary in 1914

Think

- How far is it from the east of this empire to the west?

- What problems might an emperor face in controlling his empire?

- What other empires have you studied in history?

5

The problem for Austria-Hungary was that many of the races living in the empire did not want to be ruled by Austrians. They wanted to have their own nation **states**. This is what we call **nationalism**. People who are proud of their own language, customs and achievements and who demand the right to run their own nation in their own way are called **nationalists**.

Thousands of Serbs lived in Bosnia. In 1908 the Austrians had forced Bosnia to be part of Austria-Hungary. The Serbs who lived there were furious. They wanted Bosnia to break free and to become part of Serbia, which was already an independent nation. Serbia had recently grown larger by winning land in wars in 1912 and 1913. It would dearly love to take Bosnia as well.

Think

- Which two countries might go to war with each other after the murder of the Austrian Archduke?

- What would they be fighting about?

The Austrians had no intention of giving in to Serb nationalists. If they let the Serbs have their own nation, then Poles and Czechs and others would all demand the same freedom and the whole empire might break up. But some Serbs in Bosnia showed their hatred for the Austrians by turning to violence and terrorism… which is why they murdered the Austrian Archduke in 1914.

A chain has many links.

Here are three 'links' in the chain of events leading to the First World War. Copy each one carefully onto a separate piece of paper so it can be used later in your display.

Fill in the gaps with the correct information from the section called 'Nations and empires'. There will be more links to include later!

Serb nationalists murdered the Austrian Archduke on _____ (date).

Austria-Hungary was a powerful _____ which feared it might fall apart if it gave in to nationalists in 1914.

_____ had grown in 1912 and 1913 and it wanted to join all Serbs in one nation.

Allies and enemies

As you may well have guessed, the murder of Archduke Franz Ferdinand in June 1914 led to a war between Austria-Hungary and Serbia. But it did not stop there.

The war between Serbia and Austria-Hungary spread because all the powerful empires of Europe were tied into a complicated system of **alliances**. An alliance is a partnership between two or more powers. These alliances are usually agreed by **treaties**. Often the leaders promise to defend their ally (partner) if another country attacks it.

This chart shows what happened in the six weeks following the murder of Archduke Franz Ferdinand.

How Europe's alliances helped to drag the world into war

- **28 June 1914** – Serb nationalists kill Archduke Franz Ferdinand.
- **28 July 1914** – Austria-Hungary declares war on Serbia to crush nationalism.
- **29 July 1914** – Russia prepares for war on Austria-Hungary to help her ally, Serbia.
- **1 August 1914** – Germany declares war on Russia to help her ally, Austria-Hungary.
- **2 August 1914** – France prepares for war with Germany to help her ally, Russia.
- **3 August 1914** – Germany declares war on France and attacks through Belgium.
- **4 August 1914** – Britain declares war on Germany to support her allies, Belgium and France... The First World War has begun.

The First World War lasted until November 1918. During the war other nations such as Italy (1915) and the USA (1917) entered on the side of the British. Turkey (1914) entered on the side of Germany.

Think

- What reasons might countries have for joining an alliance?
- Do you think alliances make wars more likely to happen or less likely to happen?

STEP 2

Here are three more links for you to copy and complete on separate pieces of paper. Work out from the chart which nations or empires were on which side. Hint: Who helped Serbia? Who attacked Serbia? (You will not need to mention Belgium.)

Europe's complicated system of _____ dragged all the great powers into war by 4 August 1914.

Serbia was helped by the Triple Entente alliance. It tied together these three great powers: _____ , _____ and _____ .

Serbia's enemies included the alliance of the Central Powers, _____ and _____ .

Hopes and fears

The fact that Europe's great powers were tied together in alliances is not enough to explain why there was a war. We need to go deeper to find out why different nations were rivals and enemies. This map and the fact files on the great powers will help.

France

Number of soldiers: 1.25 million

Number of battleships: 28

Money spent on arms in 1913–14: £37 million

Background information: France had lost a war against Germany in 1871. She was angry about this and wanted revenge. She also wanted to get back the land she had lost to Germany (Alsace-Lorraine). She was scared that Germany could beat her in another war if she did not have strong friends to help her. She was determined to keep her large empire, e.g. lands in Africa and Asia.

Britain

Number of soldiers: 711,000

Number of battleships: 64

Money spent on arms in 1913–14: £50 million

Background information: Britain had been the first nation to have an industrial revolution. This had made her very rich. She also had a massive empire spread across the world in places such as India, Africa, Australia and Canada. She needed to be sure that her powerful navy could control all sea routes, especially in the English Channel. She hoped that the other nations in Europe would keep each other quiet so that none of them could grow powerful enough to challenge her.

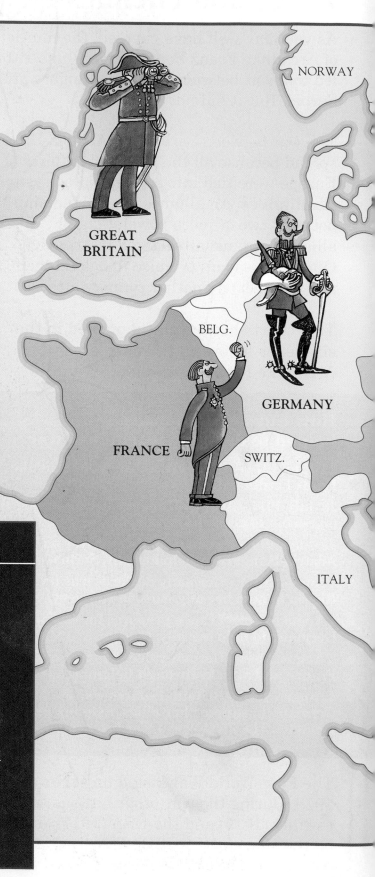

NORWAY

GREAT BRITAIN

BELG.

GERMANY

FRANCE

SWITZ.

ITALY

SWEDEN

RUSSIA

AUSTRIA-HUNGARY

SERBIA

Germany

Number of soldiers: 2.2 million

Number of battleships: 40

Money spent on arms in 1913–14: £60 million

Background information: Germany had only existed as a nation since 1871. In that year she proved that she had the strongest army in Europe when she beat France in a war and took rich areas of land from her. She was determined to catch up with Britain's wealth and power so she built many factories. From 1900 she also built many battleships. Kaiser Wilhelm, the emperor of Germany from 1888, wanted to have a world-wide empire. He also feared that Germany was being encircled by an enemy alliance.

Russia

Number of soldiers: 1.2 million

Number of battleships: 16

Money spent on arms in 1913–14: £67 million

Background information: Russia had a large empire in Asia but she wanted to have more influence over south-east Europe. This would give her access to essential supplies via the Mediterranean Sea. Austria-Hungary was a great force in south-east Europe and so was Germany. Russia had been going through hard times since 1900 and the Tsar (emperor) was unpopular. The Russian people had much in common with the Serbs and the Tsar believed his country would like him more if he supported the Serbs against Austria-Hungary.

Austria-Hungary

Number of soldiers: 810,000

Number of battleships: 16

Money spent on arms in 1913–14: £22 million

Background information: Austria-Hungary ruled over many different races, such as the Serbs, who wanted their own independent nations. The Austrians wanted to stop nationalism breaking up their large empire in central Europe. They were also scared that Russia might gain great influence in south-east Europe.

The map on pages 8–9 shows how unstable Europe was by 1914. One country's hope was another country's fear. There were several moments in the first years of the 20th century when it seemed there might be a war in Europe – but until 1914 it had always been avoided. In that year the tensions and ambitions that had been building up for years finally did erupt into war.

The chain of events leading up to the First World War goes back many years. You need to make some more links for your display. Copy each one carefully onto a separate piece of paper. Fill in the gaps with the correct information from the section called 'Hopes and fears'. Leave the links unconnected.

Since 1878 Russia had worked hard to gain allies and friends in _____ Europe by helping nationalist groups there.

All the great powers were _____ their armies and navies between 1913 and 1914.

By 1850 Britain's industry had made her rich and she was increasing her _____ to protect the sea routes to her great empire.

Germany had a new _____ in 1888 and he wanted his country to build an empire.

By 1911 Germany believed she was encircled by an _____ _____.

Germany spent a lot of money after 1900 to catch up with _____'s navy.

In 1871 Germany became a new nation after her massive army beat _____ in a bitter war.

Thinking your enquiry through

You have now made all your links. You must now organise
these to make a display about the causes of the First World War.
You can choose between two different methods.

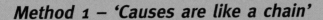

Method 1 – 'Causes are like a chain'

If you use this method you must:

a arrange your links on a large sheet of paper so that they all connect
up in the right chronological order (the order in which they happened)

b decide which links you would call short-term causes. These will
be ones which happened shortly before the war itself. Shade these
links in red

c write a short explanation about why historians use the expression
'a chain of events' when investigating causes.

Method 2 – 'Causes are like an explosive mixture'

If you use this method you must:

a use the same information but arrange it differently. Instead of
comparing causes with a chain you must show how they can be
like the ingredients of an explosive mixture such as gunpowder.
You must arrange the causes on a diagram like the one shown here.
Sort your causes into the three types shown in the picture below

b write a short explanation about why historians use the expression
'an explosive mixture' when they give the causes of some events.

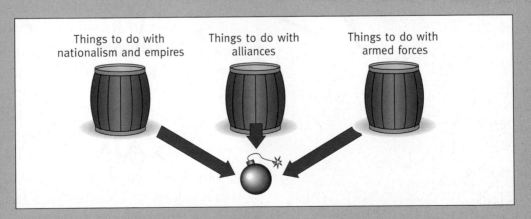

Severn and Somme

2

What can one man's letters and poems tell us about the First World War?

Ivor Gurney was brought up in Gloucester. He knew the Gloucestershire countryside very well. He and his friends liked to go for walks along the River Severn. On 9 February 1915, Gurney joined the army. Things would never be the same again.

Gurney joined a unit called the 2nd/5th Gloucesters. He wrote a letter to a friend:

It was an experience worth writing about, when we recruits stood at ease in the dusk while the 5th Gloucesters crowded around us with cries of welcome... and peered into our faces to make sure of friends. It gave me a thrill such as I have not had for a long time.

Gurney was going to fight in what we now call the First World War or the Great War. The war began in 1914. Britain's **allies** were France and Russia. Britain, France and Russia were fighting another **alliance** made up of Germany, Austria-Hungary and Italy.

Most of the fighting took place in France. Those who were going to fight in the trenches in France had to be trained. The soldiers of the 2nd/5th Gloucesters were taken to Chelmsford in Essex. This is where Gurney began his training. From Chelmsford Gurney wrote another letter.

Dear Mrs Voynich

Well, here I am, a soldier of the King! The best thing for me – at present. I feel that nowhere could I be happier than where I am (except perhaps at sea), so the experiment may be called a success.

They are good sorts, most of these boys, and will surely fight as well as those who have already gone. It is a better way to die, with these men, in such a cause <u>than the end which seemed near to me</u> just over two years ago. And if I escape, well, there will be memories for old age; not all pleasant, but <u>none so unpleasant as those which would have come if I had refused the call</u>.

Think

● Read Ivor Gurney's letters on pages 12 and 13. Find all the words and phrases which show that Gurney was happy, even excited, about the challenge ahead.

● Re-read the underlined words. Try to guess what kind of thing Gurney might be talking about.

Gurney had experienced difficulties with his nerves. He had been very depressed, even wanting to commit suicide. At that time, his condition was known as neurasthenia. This is what he is talking about in his letter. At the time of joining the army, he felt much better and hoped that being a soldier would help him to get better completely.

Gurney was a musician and composer. In 1911 he won a scholarship to study music at the Royal College of Music. He was already a very promising composer. Gurney had also begun to write poetry. He wrote this poem while he was still in training in England. He is encouraging other poets to fight bravely.

To the Poet before Battle

Now, Youth, the hour of thy dread passion comes;
Thy lovely things must all be laid away,
And thou, as others, must face the riven day
Unstirred by the tattle and rattle of rolling drums
Or bugle's strident cry. When mere noise numbs
The sense of being, the fear-sick soul doth sway;
Remember thy great craft's honour, that they may say
Nothing in shame of Poets.

Your enquiry

Poems and letters are not written for historians. Poems are not necessarily written to give a reliable account of what happened. Nor are letters. They are written for all sorts of other reasons. But if we think hard about Gurney's letters and poems we can discover a lot about his views and attitudes. We can also find out about the attitudes and experiences of other soldiers. If we use the evidence well it will tell us a complicated story of the experience of fighting in the First World War. At the end of this enquiry you will be able to challenge another imaginary writer who has not been using the evidence properly!

Think

● Gurney uses strong words in his poem like 'honour', 'passion', 'fear', and 'shame'. What does he want other poets to feel when they read this poem?

Troops in training

Here Gurney is writing to his friend, Miss Marion Scott. He was still in training in England.

16 June 1915

My dear Miss Scott

At the moment of writing, I am on the edge of a pool, watching for signs of khaki over a hedge half a mile away and cursing the army strongly.

The aim of training troops is to make them as tired as possible without teaching them anything. Take 'em for a route march, stand 'em on their heads, muck about with 'em in any fashion so long as they get tired and sick of soldiering. If you do as you are told, and have no objection to sudden death, that means a good soldier...

They are as mad as hatters here. Up at 5, Roll Call and Rifle inspection at 6. Breakfast at 6.30. Parade at 8.15. March. Dinner 1.30–2.30. Bayonet practice 3.30. Tea 4.30.

Think

- Which of these words describe Gurney's mood in this letter: amused, cross, disrespectful, humorous, angry, irritated, relaxed?

- What does this source tell you about how troops were trained?

- What does it tell you about Gurney's attitude to training?

To the trenches

But

Most of the fighting in the First World War took place in Belgium and France. By the end of 1914 millions of troops were dug into a long line of trenches which stretched from the North Sea to the Alps.

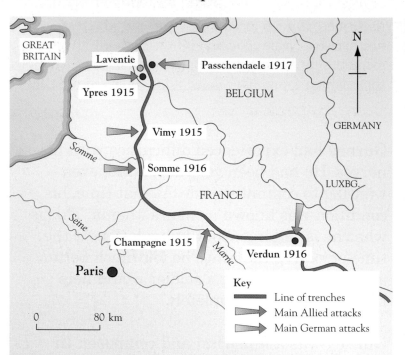

Trenches and battles of the First World War

The 2nd/5th Gloucesters arrived in France on 25 May 1916. Bit by bit they moved towards Laventie. They reached Laventie on 10 June. It was only a mile or so from the front-line.

Soldiers in France were either 'in the line', 'in reserve' or 'at rest' in some camp many miles from the fighting lines. When Gurney and the Gloucesters arrived at Laventie they were in the second of these roles – 'in reserve'. Their jobs were:

- to supply rations to the front-line
- to supply working parties for the front-line
- to garrison the reserve posts.

When, later, they were in the front-line, their trench would have looked something like this.

Whatever their duties, soldiers spent a lot of time doing quite boring tasks. They had to carry out endless 'fatigues': repairing trenches and wiring, moving rations and stores, cleaning, clearing, bringing in the wounded and burying the dead. Gurney describes this in a letter to Marion Scott:

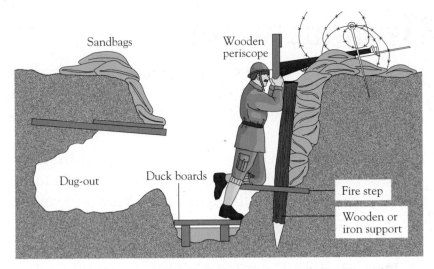

Cross-section of a front-line trench

25 October 1916

My dear friend,

I promised to tell you something of my life in the trenches. Our last orders were as follows: Stand To 5.30. Stand Down, clean rifles 6.00. Breakfast 7.30. Work 8.30–12.30. Dinner 1. Tea 4.30. Stand To 5.–5.30. Stand Down. Then Ration Fatigue. Listening Post. Sentry. Wiring Party. Some of these last all night. One is allowed to sleep off duty – but not in the dugouts and the average, now the cold weather has come, and rain, is about three hours sleep. Out of trenches there are parades, inspections, chiefly for shortages; and fatigues... the life is as grey as it sounds, but one manages to hang on to life by watching the cheerier spirits – wonderful people some of them; after all, it is better to be depressed with reason than without.

...Here there are nine men in a tiny dugout; but good fires and we manage a hot drink three or four times every day!

Think

- Choose words and phrases from Gurney's letter which show that life in the trenches was miserable.

- Choose words and phrases which show how some soldiers stayed cheerful.

What do Ivor Gurney's letters and poems tell us about:

Gurney's personality?	Gurney's experiences in the trenches?	Gurney's attitude to the war?	Other people's attitudes and experiences?

Copy this table. Choose short examples from Gurney's poems and letters to go under each heading. Go right back to the beginning of the enquiry and use all the letters and poems that you have read so far.

With the Welsh

In February 1916 the Germans began a battle to capture French forts around Verdun (find it on the map on page 14). By July 1916 about 700,000 men had fallen. The **Allies** were close to defeat.

Gurney's 2nd/5th Gloucesters were spared this horror. They did not leave the Laventie line until the end of October. We learn very little about what was happening in Verdun from Gurney's letters.

His letters during the summer of 1916 are very calm. He keeps a distance from the war's events. You could even call his letters happy! The next two letters help to explain why.

7 June 1916

Dear Miss Scott

Your letter has just reached me, here, dans les tranchées. Where and How I may not say; bang in the front seat we are. ... But O what luck! Here am I in a signal dugout with some of the nicest young men I have ever met. And would you believe it? My luck I mean; they talk their native language and sing their own folksongs with sweet and natural voices. I did not sleep at all for the first day in my dugout – there was too much to be said, asked, experienced. It was one of the most notable evenings of my life.

These few days in the signal dugout with my Welsh friends are of the happiest for years. ... War's damned interesting. It would be hard indeed to be deprived of all this now, when my mind is becoming saner and more engaged with outside things. It is not hard for me to die, but a thing sometimes unbearable to leave this life; and God makes these Welsh into fine gentlemen. It would seem that War is one of his ways of doing so. Best wishes for health

Yours very sincerely, Ivor Gurney

P.S. Yesterday in the trenches... there was a trench mortar attack, and we had casualties. As I was in the Signallers' dugout, a bombardment means little else but noise – as yet. But a whiz-bang missed me and a tin of Machonachie (my dinner) by ten yards; a shower of dirt, no more. Good luck to us all. The Welsh sang 'David of the White Rock' and the 'Slumber Song'. And O their voices! I thank God for the experience.

Think

- Find examples in this letter of Gurney's love of music, and of his happiness.

- Find examples in this letter of danger.

- There are no signs of fear in this letter. Do you think that this is because Gurney does not choose to write about it? Or do you think that it is because he was not at all afraid?

Here is an extract from another letter, about exactly the same experience, but written to a different person. It is a letter to Catherine Abercrombie, written on the same day, 7 June 1916:

We talked of Welsh folksong, of George Borrow, of Burns; of – yes – of Oscar Wilde, Shakespeare, and of the war; distant from us by 300 yards. Snipers were continually firing, and rockets – fairy lights they call them: fired from a pistol – lit up the night outside. Every now and again a distant rumble of guns to remind us the reason we are gathered. They spoke of their friends dead or maimed in the bombardment the night before, and in the face of their grief I sat there, and for once, self-forgetful.

... Once we were standing outside our dugout, when a cuckoo sounded its call from the shattered wood at the back. What could I think of but Framilode, Minsterworth, Cranham, and the old haunts of home.

Think

● Framilode, Minsterworth and Cranham are all places in Gloucestershire. What reminded Gurney of these places?

● What do you think Gurney means by saying 'in the face of their grief I sat there ... self-forgetful'?

After the war was over, Gurney wrote a poem called 'First Time In'. It was about that first evening spent with the Welsh. He calls the evening, 'That strangely beautiful entry to war's rout'. Now that you have read his letters, you will know what he means. Here is part of that poem:

First Time In
                          ... the divine
Afterglow brought us up to a Welsh colony
Hiding in sandbag ditches, whispering consolatory
Soft foreign things. Then we were taken in
To low huts candle-lit, shaded close by slitten
Oilsheets, and there the boys gave us kind welcome,
So that we looked out as from the edge of home.
Sang us Welsh things, and changed all former notions
To human hopeful things. And the next day's guns
Nor any line-pangs ever quite could blot out
That strangely beautiful entry to war's rout ...
'David of the White Rock', the 'Slumber Song' so soft, and that
Beautiful tune to which roguish words by Welsh pit boys
Are sung – but never more beautiful than there under the guns' noise.

Think

● How do Gurney's letters help you to understand what he means by 'whispering consolatory soft foreign things' and 'sang us Welsh things'?

● What do you think he means by 'never more beautiful than there under the guns' noise'?

1 Add more points and examples to the table you began in Step 1.

2 Underline or shade in yellow anything that shows a contrast or change from the conclusions you reached at the end of Step 1.

He's gone

This letter was written in August 1916, shortly after Gurney heard news that his best friend from Gloucestershire, Will Harvey, had been killed:

24 August 1916

My dear Miss Scott

... Willy Harvey, my best friend, went out on patrol a week ago, and never came back... We were firm in friendship and I will never look for a closer bond. He was nobly unselfish at most times, and all who knew him and understood him, must not merely have liked him, but loved him... As a soldier, or as a man, he was dauntlessly brave. His desire for nobility and sacrifice was unquenchable, and was, at last, his doom. We desired a better ending for him than a sniper's bullet in No Mans Land.

If I live to a great age, nothing can alter my memory of him or the evenings we spent together at Minsterworth. My thoughts of Bach and all firelit frosty evenings will be full of him, and the perfectest evening of Autumn will but recall him the more vividly to my memory. He is my friend, and nothing can alter that. If I have the good fortune ever to meet with such another, he has a golden memory to contend with.

To His Love

He's gone, and all our plans
Are useless indeed.
We'll walk no more on Cotswold
Where the sheep feed
Quietly and take no heed.

His body that was so quick
Is not as you
Knew it, on Severn river
Under the blue
Driving our small boat through.

You would not know him now...
But still he died
Nobly, so cover him over
With violets of pride
Purple from Severn side.

Cover him, cover him soon!
And with thick-set
Masses of memoried flowers–
Hide that red wet
Thing I must somehow forget.

STEP 3

1 Add more points and examples to the table you began in Step 1.

2 Underline or shade in yellow anything that shows a contrast or change from the conclusions you reached at the end of Step 2.

It turned out that Will Harvey was not dead. He had been captured by the Germans. He was to outlive Gurney by 30 years.

More like rats than men: winter on the Somme

These British soldiers are running across No Mans Land in between the Allied and the German front-lines. Most of them would have been killed. This was the Battle of the Somme.

Field Marshal Douglas Haig planned the attack on the Somme in order to relieve the pressure on Verdun. After a week-long **artillery** bombardment of German trenches, British troops advanced.

It was a terrible disaster. On the first day there were 57,000 British casualties. The fighting continued until November 1916 with the loss of one-and-a-quarter million men.

The 2nd/5th Gloucesters missed most of the slaughter. They remained in the fairly quiet area of Laventie until 27 October 1916. They then began a slow trek southwards to join in the last days of the Battle of the Somme.

As Gurney and the 2nd/5th Gloucesters approached the Somme, they would have noticed a big contrast with the trenches at Laventie. The conditions on the Somme were very basic. There was mud, deep enough to submerge a large gun. Unburied dead were strewn over the battlefields. In places, there was no sign of organised trenches, just shell holes joined up to one another.

By 22 November 1916 the 2nd/5th Gloucesters were in position and ready for action. It was from here that Gurney wrote a letter to Marion Scott:

> 7 December 1916
>
> My dear friend, we suffer pain out here, and for myself it sometimes seems that death would be preferable to such a life. Yet my chief thought is that I have found myself unfitted for Life and Battle, and am gradually being strengthened and made fit for some high task.

They remained 'in the line', on and off, until 24 December. Then, on 30 December, they moved on to Varennes. It was the coldest winter in living memory.

Think

- Find Laventie and the river Somme on the map on page 14.

- Use the scale to work out how far the 2nd/5th Gloucesters travelled on their journey to the Somme.

We shall never make a soldier out of you

During that winter, Gurney found it very difficult to stick to army rules on cleanliness and smart appearance.

3 February 1917

My Dear Friend

... But O, the cleaning up! I suppose I get as much hell as anyone in the army; and although I give the same time to cleaning as any of the others, the results are not all they might be. Today there was an inspection by the Colonel. I waited trembling, knowing there was six weeks of dirt and rust not yet all off; no, not by a long way. I stood there, and waited for the bolt and thunder. Round came He-Who-Must-Be-Obeyed, looked at me, hesitated, and was called off by the R.S.M. who was afterwards heard telling the Colonel, 'Quite a good man, sir, but he's a musician, and doesn't seem able to get himself clean.' When the R.S.M. came round, he chuckled and said, 'Ah Gurney, I'm afraid we shall never make a soldier out of you.'... the R.S.M. is a brick.

'Hell', a painting of the First World War, by George Leroux

This poem, 'Pain', was written in February 1917:

Pain, pain continual; pain unending;
Hard even to the roughest, but to those
Hungry for beauty... <u>Grey monotony</u> lending
Weight to the <u>grey skies, grey mud</u> where goes
An army of <u>grey bedrenched scarecrows</u> in rows
Careless at last of cruellest Fate-sending.
Seeing the pitiful eyes of men foredone,
Or horses shot, too tired merely to stir,
Dying in shell-holes both, <u>slain by the mud</u>.
Men broken, shrieking even to hear a gun.
Till pain grinds down, or lethargy numbs her,
The amazed heart cries angrily out on God.

Think

● Read the poem 'Pain' again very carefully. Which details in the painting 'Hell' does the poem also describe?

Think

● From these three letters what kinds of things would you say were worrying or concerning Gurney at this time?

Following the German retreat

Early in March 1917 the Gloucesters began to follow the German retreat. The Germans were retreating to their new, stronger positions, called the Hindenburg line.

23 March 1917

Dear Miss Scott
Things are beginning to move and no one knows when may come the next opportunity for writing. I have just received your letter of March 11th... The German retreat may mean little letter writing.

25 March 1917

Dear Howler
I see in today's Daily Mail that food regulations are to be made more strict. Is it really serious? What a time our poor villagers must be having! I don't like to think of some of my Framilode friends, to whom the price of bread is a real distress.

26 March 1917

Dear Miss Scott
On the march, not many days ago, we passed a ruined garden, and there were snowdrops. Snowdrops, the first flowers I had seen for so long. So I plucked one for each for my friends that I so desire to see again, and one for Gloucestershire...

The Germans had done things very thoroughly as they withdrew. Villages were destroyed. All fruit trees were cut down. All cross-roads were mined. All wells were destroyed or poisoned. This made it hard for the 2nd/5th Gloucesters who were following them.

21

Near Vermand

Lying flat on my belly <u>shivering in clutch-frost</u>,
There was time to watch the stars, we had dug in:
Looking eastward over the low ridge; <u>March scurried its
    blast</u>
<u>At our senses</u>, no use either dying or struggling.
Low woods to left (Cotswold her spinnies if ever!)
Showed through snow flurries and the clearer star weather,
And nothing but chill and wonder lived in mind; nothing
But loathing and fine beauty, and <u>wet loathed clothing</u>.
Here were thoughts. <u>Cold smothering and fire-desiring</u>,
A day to follow like this or in the digging or wiring.
<u>Worry in snow flurrying and lying flat, flesh the earth
    loathing</u>.
I was the forward sentry and would be relieved
In a quarter or so, but nothing more better than to crouch
Low in the scraped holes and to have <u>frozen and rocky couch</u>
To be by <u>desperate home thoughts</u> clutched at, and
    heart-grieved.

Think

- What feelings and experiences does Gurney share in this poem, that he did not reveal in his letters? The underlined words will help you.

STEP 4

1 Re-read pages 19, 20 and 21. Add more points and examples to the table you began in Step 1.

2 Underline or shade in yellow anything that shows a contrast or change from the conclusions you reached at the end of Step 3.

Passchendaele

On Good Friday, Gurney was wounded. A bullet went through his right arm. He stayed in hospital for about six weeks. His letters show that he was back in the fighting by 30 May, but his job was changed. He was transferred to the machine guns.

At the end of July 1917, Field Marshal Sir Douglas Haig began a new attack. This was the Third Battle of Ypres. Heavy rain created night-mare conditions around the ruined village of Passchendaele. The soldiers were soon hopelessly bogged down.

By the middle of August the 2nd/5th Gloucesters were on the march to join them.

The photograph gives you some idea of the conditions at Passchendaele.

We do not know the part that Gurney played in the Third Battle of Ypres. Not much survives to tell us about Gurney's experiences. We do know that during the battle he was gassed. It was not serious, and Gurney recovered. He was sent to hospital in Scotland. It was the end of Gurney's war.

How the First World War ended

The war had been going on at sea as well as on land. The Germans had been attacking and destroying American ships which they suspected of carrying supplies to the Allies. They also sank passenger ships, killing many American **civilians**. The USA finally declared war on Germany on 1 April 1917.

The German situation was desperate by early 1918. The Allies' blockade of German ports had starved German industry of raw materials, and starved the population of food.

The Germans made one last, big push. This was called the Ludendorff Offensive. It was doomed to fail. German advances were held up as troops stopped to loot food from captured trenches or villages. The best of the German troops had been killed on the battlefields of Verdun or the Somme. Between May and August the Germans made no further progress.

By October the Germans were in full retreat. On 11 November 1918 the hell of the First World War was over…

But Ivor Gurney's hell had hardly begun.

Strange hells for Ivor Gurney

The First World War made Ivor Gurney into a very successful poet. In October 1917, 46 poems were published in a book called *Severn and Somme*. It received very good reviews.

Even before the end of the war, Gurney's mental health went downhill. Whilst in France, he had been well. In 1918 he had a complete breakdown. Many of his letters were about suicide. In October 1918 he was discharged. They called it 'shell-shock'. It was probably more complicated than that.

In May 1919 another book of poems, *War's Embers*, was published. Gurney got a little better. During the two or three years after the war he produced some of his best music and poems.

It was at this time that he wrote 'Strange Hells':

Strange Hells

There are strange hells in the minds war
   made …
As one would have expected – the racket
   and the fear guns made.
One hell the Gloucester soldiers they quite
   put out:
Their first bombardment, when in combined
   black shout
Of fury, guns aligned, they ducked lower
   their heads
And sang with diaphragms fixed beyond all
   dreads,
That tin and stretched-wire tinkle, that
   blither of tune:
'Après la guerre fini', till all hell had come
   down,
Twelve-inch, six-inch, and eighteen
   pounders hammering hell's thunders.

Then things got worse again. Gurney took various unsuccessful jobs in London and in Gloucestershire: cinema pianist, work in a cold-storage depot, tax clerk, work on a farm. Nothing seemed to settle his mind. There were growing signs of disturbance. He hardly slept, he went on long, night walks, he was completely unreliable, he seemed confused and he was often distressed.

In September 1922 he was sent to a mental hospital at Gloucester. In December 1922 he moved to the City of London Mental Hospital at Dartford, Kent. He never left it.

Think

- Pick out all the words and phrases in this poem that are about noise.

Thinking your enquiry through

In history we have to write generalisations. We have to sum things up. When we are summing things up, it is very easy to make things far too simple. As you have seen, Ivor Gurney's story is complicated. The evidence needs to be handled with care.

Here are three **generalisations** written by an imaginary, textbook author. You must use the evidence to challenge each one. Write a heading: <u>A complicated story</u>. Copy out each generalisation. Then write a few sentences, supported with examples of evidence from Gurney's poems and letters, to explain why the generalisation is too simple. We have started you off!

Generalisation 1 Ivor Gurney really enjoyed the First World War.	**Too simple!** True, there is a lot of evidence to show that he was healthier and happier than ever before, but there is also a lot of evidence to show that he found the war disturbing and terrifying. One example is …
Generalisation 2 Ivor Gurney hated being in the trenches.	**Too simple!** True, his poems capture the horror of it, but there were times when he found happiness that he had never known before. For example, …
Generalisation 3 Ivor Gurney's letters and poems can only tell us about Ivor Gurney.	**Too simple!** True, they are probably most reliable for the attitudes and views of Ivor Gurney, but go back to each of your Steps. Gurney's letters and poems also gave a wider picture. They tell us about …

It is difficult to say whether the war made his mental health worse or better. Either way, he never recovered. He died in December 1937 and was buried in his beloved Gloucestershire.

From 1938 onwards his music and poems began to receive great praise. Ivor Gurney had become a 'war poet'.

Severn Meadows

Only the wanderer
Knows England's graces
Or can anew see clear
Familiar faces

And who loves Joy as he
That dwells in shadows?
Do not forget me quite,
O Severn meadows.

Ivor Gurney, 1916

'Are we making a good peace? Are we? Are we?'

Did the Paris peace conference make a sensible settlement?

On 28 June 1919, exactly five years after the murders at Sarajevo which had sparked off the First World War, the most powerful men in the world and their chief advisers met in a magnificent palace just outside Paris. This painting was made soon afterwards to record the event.

The men and their chief advisers gathered in the famous Hall of Mirrors at the Palace of Versailles. The leaders watched in silence as the German representatives entered the room, walked slowly to the long table where the treaty lay, sat down and signed the papers.

'The signing of the Treaty of Versailles in the Hall of Mirrors' painted by William Orpen in 1919

In the months that followed, **treaties** were signed by the other defeated nations. These agreements were supposed to restore the world to a path of peace and security. But no one was sure that they would work. The problems faced by the politicians were very deep and there had been many arguments about what the treaties should say. One British adviser, Harold Nicolson, recorded his worries in his diary. 'Are we making a good peace?' he asked. 'Are we? Are we?'

Only time would tell.

Your enquiry

In this enquiry you must take on the role of one of the diplomats (advisers) at the peace conference. You will have to wrestle with the problems that confronted the politicians in 1919. And you will have to face up to your own doubts and worries about the peace settlements. Just like Harold Nicolson, you will keep a diary of your thoughts and feelings at each stage.

Problems, problems

When the politicians met in Paris they faced many problems. There were four in particular:

Problem 1: The war had brought massive destruction, especially to buildings and farming land in France. How could all this damage be repaired?

Problem 2: From eastern Europe to Ireland and throughout the world, **nationalist** groups were keener than ever to rule themselves and to be free from the **empires** which had controlled them.

Problem 3: Communists had taken over in Russia in 1917. Their ideas were spreading to other countries that had suffered greatly in the war. Communists believed that the poor should rise up and take power from the rich. The people in power were scared!

Problem 4: The First World War had cost twenty million lives. The world had never seen a war like it. How could future wars be prevented?

Think

- Which of these problems do you think it was most important to deal with?

Over one thousand politicians and **diplomats** came to the peace conference to decide what should be done. But the leaders of three countries were really in charge. These three countries were the USA, Great Britain and France. Together they were known as The Big Three. Their leaders knew exactly what they wanted.

The USA was represented by its **President**, Woodrow Wilson. These were his main ideas:

The war started in 1914 because some nations were scared that secret **alliances** had been made against them. There must be no more secret treaties between countries.

Every nation must reduce the number of its weapons. The **arms race** led us into the last war.

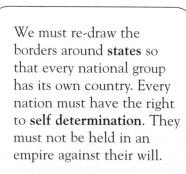

We must re-draw the borders around **states** so that every national group has its own country. Every nation must have the right to **self determination**. They must not be held in an empire against their will.

Think

● What was self determination?

● What was the League of Nations?

Finally I want to see a new organisation which will end quarrels between countries without war. It will be called the 'League of Nations'. It will help enemies to talk through their problems and to solve disputes peacefully.

Britain was represented by its **Prime Minister**, David Lloyd George.
Here are his main ideas:

Every national group from the broken empires of Germany and Austria-Hungary must have the right to rule itself freely.

We must keep the British Empire strong, united and well defended.

The Germans must be made to pay for the damage they caused in this war (but I secretly worry what will happen if we treat them too harshly).

Britain is a trading nation. We must quickly build up our trade links with other countries – including Germany.

Think

- Why do you think Lloyd George was worried about being too harsh on the Germans?

France was represented by its Prime Minister, Georges Clemenceau.
Here are his main ideas:

We must force Germany to pay France all she needs to repair the damage caused by the war

We must make Germany so weak that she will never dare to attack France again.

The Germans must be made to admit to the world that they alone caused the war.

We must take revenge on Germany for humiliating us in earlier wars and for the suffering she has caused in this one.

Think

- What do all Clemenceau's ideas have in common?

STEP 1

Work in threes. One of you is a diplomat advising Wilson (USA). Another is advising Lloyd George (Britain). The third is advising Clemenceau (France).

Write a short summary of each of the main points your leader has made. After each one say which of the four problems on page 27 you think his idea may solve.

If you are the diplomat advising Clemenceau your first entry could look like this:

Clemenceau wants revenge on Germany. He hopes this will stop another war.

Decisions, decisions

On these two pages you can see thirteen of the main choices facing the politicians. Meet the diplomats from the other two countries and discuss each problem carefully. Decide what you will advise your leaders. The map will help you. Try to make your decision fit with your leader's aims as shown on page 28 or 29. Note down each decision briefly in your diary.

All three diplomats in your group must agree on each decision before you move on. You will not always get your own way!

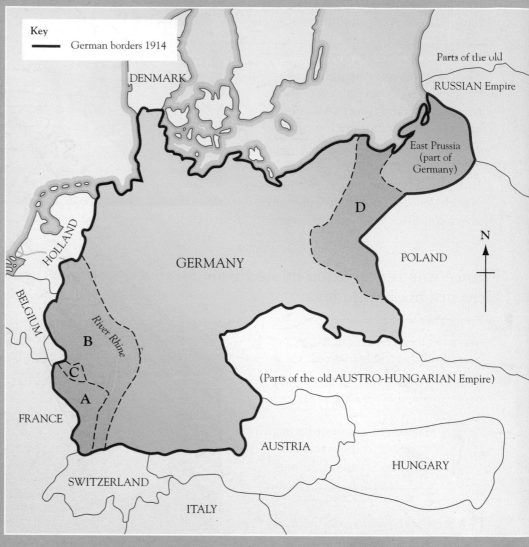

Europe in 1919 – problem areas considered at the peace conference

1 Area A on the map marks Alsace-Lorraine. Germany took this area from France in 1871. Should you:
   a return it to France?
   b let Germany keep it?

2 Area B on the map is the Rhineland. It is the place from which Germany can most easily attack France. Should you:
   a let Germany keep it as before?
   b let Germany keep it but insist that she never puts any soldiers in this border area?

3 Area C on the map is the Saarland. It is an important coal-mining part of Germany. Should you:

a let it be run by the League of Nations for fifteen years and allow France to have all its coal in those years?

b give it to France forever?

4 Area D on the map is part of Germany. Most people there are Germans but some are Poles. You want to make the new nation, Poland, as strong as possible. Should you:

a give this land to Poland and split Germany in two?

b let Germany keep it?

5 You guess that Germany and Austria (see map) may want to join to become one country. They share the same language and culture. Should you:

a forbid them to join as one nation?

b allow them to join as one nation?

6 Should you:

a allow Germany to keep a full army, navy and air force?

b order Germany to cut down drastically on all her armed forces?

7 Should you:

a let the League of Nations run Germany's overseas colonies?

b give Germany's colonies to Britain and France?

8 Should you:

a fine Germany a large sum of money to pay for the damage done in the war?

b fine Germany a massive sum of money to pay for damage done in the war?

9 Should you:

a leave any mention of guilt or blame for the war out of the treaty?

b make Germany sign a War Guilt Clause accepting all blame for starting the war?

10 Austria-Hungary has been united as one for many years. Should you:

a let them continue as one country?

b force them to split into two countries?

11 There are many national groups scattered around the old empire of Austria-Hungary. Should you:

a create lots of small new nations?

b create one or two strong new nations, even if this means grouping different national groups together?

12 The League of Nations is going to be set up to help nations solve problems by talking. Should you:

a let all nations join?

b let all nations join except the ones who lost in the world war and Russia which has gone communist?

13 The League of Nations must be respected and have authority. Should you:

a let the League of Nations have an army made up of soldiers from all members?

b let the League of Nations have no army at all?

Surprise, surprise

The conference is coming to a close. The politicians have considered the advice that you provided and they have reached their joint decisions. Some of their agreements may surprise you – or maybe they accepted all your advice. See for yourself by checking this map and the lists that follow. They show some of the actual terms of the treaties made in Paris.

Key
- New countries
- De-militarised Rhineland
- Alsace-Lorraine (French gain)
- The Saar

Europe after the Paris peace conference

From the Treaty of Versailles with Germany

- Alsace-Lorraine must be returned to France.
- No German troops are to be allowed in the Rhineland, but it remains part of Germany.
- The Saarland is to be run for fifteen years by the League of Nations. In that time France will keep all coal mined there.
- Poland will be given the extra strip of land which means that Germany will now be split into two parts. (The land became known as the Polish Corridor.)
- Germany and Austria must never unite as one country.
- Germany must drastically cut her armed forces. She may keep only 100,000 soldiers in her army, only six battleships in the navy and she must have no air force.
- Germany's **colonies** are to be given to the League of Nations (which will then allow countries like France and Britain to look after them).
- Germany must pay a massive sum of money to pay for war damage. This is to be known as **reparations**. (In 1920 the figure was set at £6,600 million!)
- Germany had to accept full blame for starting the war.

From the Treaty of St Germain with Austria (1919) and the Treaty of Trianon with Hungary (1920)

- Austria-Hungary is to be split into two separate nations forever.
- Two large new nations are to be created from land belonging to the old Austria-Hungary. These nations are Czechoslovakia and Yugoslavia.

General Agreements

- No defeated nation or Russia may join the League of Nations.
- The League of Nations will not have an army of any sort.

Think

- You may have noticed that the defeated nations such as Germany, Austria and Hungary were not allowed to speak for themselves at the conference. Why do you think they were not allowed to attend?

- How helpful would it have been to allow the defeated nations to attend the conference?

STEP 3

Remember that you are in role as a diplomat for the USA, Britain or France.

1 Check the decisions made by the politicians against the ones you made in Step 2. On your list, place a tick next to each one where they did what you advised. Place a cross next to the ones where they ignored your advice.

2 Now go back through your list. This time do not just think about what your country wanted at the conference. This time you must be as honest with yourself as Harold Nicolson was when he asked, 'Are we making a good peace? Are we? Are we?' Take a coloured pencil or highlighter and mark any decisions which you think may be foolish or dangerous for the future of Europe and the world.

Thinking your enquiry through

Remembering that you are still in role as a diplomat, write a final, honest, diary entry about the peace settlement. Use the notes and coloured markings you have made in your diary so far (in Steps 1, 2 and 3) to help you.

1 Sum up whether you think your nation got what it wanted out of the peace settlement.

2 Choose the three things which worry you most about the peace settlement and explain why you fear they may cause trouble in later years.

Postscript

You may be interested to read this short extract from another page in Harold Nicolson's diary. He wrote it in June 1919, just before the signing of the Treaty of Versailles in the Hall of Mirrors:

There is not a single person among the younger people here who is not unhappy with the terms of the treaty. If I were the Germans, I wouldn't sign it for a moment.

But the Germans did sign. They had to. Their army had been crushed and their fleet had been sunk. They had no way of fighting back... until later.

Revolution ④

Why were the Russians so divided in 1917?

This is a photograph of the Tsar of Russia and his family in 1913. The Russian empire over which Tsar Nicholas II ruled was huge. It stretched for more than 4000 miles from east to west. Around 130 million people lived within its borders. In February 1913 Tsar Nicholas II and his people celebrated 300 years of rule by the Romanovs – the Tsar's family. St Petersburg, the capital, buzzed with excitement. Important visitors filled the hotels. The inhabitants of the city decorated the streets in the imperial colours of red, white and blue. They covered statues of the Tsar and his ancestors in ribbons and flowers.

Nicholas II hoped that his family would continue to rule Russia for many centuries to come. He was wrong. The Tsar's rule lasted only four more years. During the First World War Russian people became angry and bitter as millions of their soldiers were killed. At home the war caused terrible shortages. Many ordinary Russians could not afford to keep warm or to feed their families.

By March 1917 people were desperate. Thousands of workers in St Petersburg once again filled the streets. This time they demonstrated against the government. The **Tsar's** troops refused to fire on the people and joined in the demonstrations. This was now a **revolution**.

Think

- Why do you think the soldiers refused to fire on the people?
- What is the difference between a demonstration and a revolution?

On 16 March Nicholas II **abdicated**. A new Provisional Government took control of Russia. All across the Russian empire people rejoiced at the end of the monarchy. In St Petersburg statues of the tsars were smashed to pieces.

A photograph of children in St Petersburg looking at the head of a statue of one of the Tsars

But the revolution was not yet over. In April 1917 this man returned to Russia:

His name was Lenin and he was the leader of a political **party** called the **Bolsheviks**. Lenin and the Bolsheviks were followers of **communism**. They believed that:

- everyone should have an equal share in Russia's wealth
- peasants should have a share of the land
- workers should own a share of the factory where they worked
- the war should be ended immediately.

In October 1917 the Bolsheviks seized power from the Provisional Government. Lenin and his party then began their work of transforming Russia into the world's first **communist state**.

Your enquiry

Not everyone in Russia supported the Bolsheviks in 1917. Russians were bitterly divided. In the years between 1918 and 1921 there was a bloody civil war between the supporters and opponents of communism. In this enquiry you will find out why Russian people were so divided in 1917.

Bolsheviks into power

It was on the evening of 25 October 1917 that the Bolsheviks seized power from the Provisional Government in St Petersburg.

This painting shows the Bolsheviks 'storming' the Winter Palace. Inside were the government ministers and their soldiers.

Think

- Think of some words to describe the mood captured by this painting.

- How can you tell from the painting that the artist supported the Bolsheviks?

A painting made in Russia in the 1930s showing the storming of the Winter Palace

The picture portrays the Bolsheviks as great heroes who fought hard to capture the Winter Palace. In fact, we now know that the October Revolution was a shambles. Some of the sailors who were expected to help the Bolsheviks arrived late. The huge field guns, like the one in the picture, were too rusty to fire. No one could find the red lantern which was to signal the start of the attack.

The Bolsheviks only succeeded in 1917 because hardly anyone came to the support of the Provisional Government. Even some of the soldiers in the Winter Palace decided to slip away. Instead of fighting they went to eat their evening meals in the restaurants of St Petersburg.

STEP 1

Work in pairs.
One of you is a supporter of the Bolsheviks.
The other is an opponent.

Supporter
Write three sentences to sum up why the October Revolution was something to be proud of.

Opponent
Write three sentences to sum up why the October Revolution was nothing to be proud of.

A one-party state

The Bolsheviks seized power easily, but they were not yet in control. Many people opposed the new government. From the very beginning of the new regime, Lenin set out to destroy all opposition parties.

Bolshevik soldiers smashed up the offices of opposition newspapers and arrested their editors.

Lenin's new secret police force, the Cheka, tortured and executed opponents of his new government.

The Provisional Government had promised the people that there would be an election to decide who should represent them in a new Constituent Assembly (parliament). Lenin was forced to go ahead with this election in November 1917. But the Bolsheviks did badly and were outnumbered in the Constituent Assembly. Lenin had no intention of losing power. He was determined to make Russia communist. In January 1918 he sent his soldiers to the Constituent Assembly and closed it down. Russia had become a **one-party state**.

A painting of the Bolsheviks closing the Constituent Assembly, made in 1922

STEP 2

Supporter
Write three sentences to sum up how the new government gained control of Russia. Write a fourth sentence to explain why these actions were necessary.

Opponent
Write three sentences to sum up how the Bolsheviks crushed their opponents. Write a fourth sentence to explain why you are so shocked and angered by this.

The peace

After the October Revolution the Russian people were desperate for peace with Germany. The war had caused enough suffering. In November 1917 a group of Bolshevik **diplomats** travelled to Brest Litovsk to begin peace talks. The Germans made very harsh demands. Lenin was afraid that if a peace treaty was not signed German troops would capture Petrograd (which was the new name for St Petersburg). The Germans would then remove the Bolsheviks from power. In March 1918 the two sides finally signed the Treaty of Brest Litovsk.

Many Russians felt that the Treaty of Brest Litovsk brought a shameful peace. This map shows the huge amount of territory which Russia was forced to give up. Included in this territory was:

- 34% of Russia's population
- 32% of Russia's agricultural land
- 54% of Russia's factories
- 89% of Russia's coal-mines.

Think

- How would each of these losses weaken Russia?

STEP 3

Supporter
Explain why you think it was necessary to sign the Treaty of Brest Litovsk in 1917.

Opponent
Explain why you think the Bolsheviks were wrong to sign the Treaty of Brest Litovsk.

Key

Land lost in Treaty of Brest Litovsk

0   500 km

FINLAND

Petrograd

Moscow

Brest Litovsk

RUSSIA

UKRAINE

ROMANIA

Black Sea

Caspian Sea

TURKEY

A map showing territory lost in the Treaty of Brest Litovsk

Fair shares

The communists knew that if they were to remain in power they had to keep the promises which they had made to the Russian people. During the autumn and winter of 1917 they passed a number of decrees which aimed to make Russia a more equal society.

- Women were declared equal to men.
- Peasants who had a surplus of grain were forced to hand it over to the government so that people in the cities would have enough bread.
- Factories were taken away from their owners and placed under the control of workers' committees.
- All land was taken away from the Tsar and the old landlords.
- A maximum 48-hour working week was declared for factory workers.
- Money and jewellery in rich people's bank accounts were taken by the state.
- Rich people were forced to share their houses with poor families.

Many rich and educated people escaped from the new regime. For many of those who stayed life became unbearable. Ordinary Russians were rude and hostile towards them. Armed gangs raided their houses. **Aristocrats**, factory directors, lawyers, artists, priests and teachers were rounded up. They were forced to do jobs like clearing rubbish and snow from the streets.

A photograph of wealthy Russians clearing rubbish in the streets

Think

- Do these changes make you think that Russia was becoming a fairer society?

STEP 4

Supporter
List three important ways in which the Bolsheviks tried to create a more equal society in Russia.

Opponent
List three reasons why some people would be angry about this communist system.

Execution

After the abdication of the Tsar in March 1917 the members of the Romanov family – the royal family – were placed under house arrest. To the Bolsheviks they were a symbol of centuries of unfair government. In a palace near St Petersburg they spent their days reading, gardening, rowing and playing tennis – but they had no power. Guards patrolled the garden to make sure that they could not leave.

Think

- Do you think the Tsar and his family would want to escape from this captivity?
- Which people might want to help the Tsar to escape?

The Romanovs soon became a big problem for the Bolshevik government. The Bolsheviks feared that if the Tsar escaped he might help the opponents of the new regime. In the early months of 1918 there were rumours of plots to free the **imperial** family. The communists moved the Romanovs to a town called Ekaterinburg in the Ural mountains. It was there that the royal family would die.

On the night of 16 July 1918, secret police officers awoke the Tsar and Tsarina together with their five children. They told them to move into the cellar. They said that there was unrest in the town and that the members of the royal family were unsafe in their bedrooms. When the Romanovs were all in the cellar the officers opened fire. Bullets ricocheted off the stone walls. Blood covered the floor. When the shooting stopped and the smoke cleared two of the children were still alive. They were finished off with bayonets and bullets to the head.

The corpses were driven off in a lorry. The officers wanted to throw them down a deep mine shaft, but on the way the lorry got stuck in mud. Instead, the royal family were buried in the ground. The soldiers poured sulphuric acid on the faces of the dead family so that they could not be recognised.

For many years afterwards the communist government insisted that the decision to murder the Romanovs was made by the local Bolsheviks in Ekaterinburg. We now know that the orders came from the communist leadership in Moscow.

A photograph of the room in which the murder of the royal family took place

Supporter

Write two sentences to explain why you think the murder of the Tsar and his family was acceptable.

Opponent

Write two sentences to explain why you think the murder of the Tsar and his family was such a shameful thing to do.

Thinking your enquiry through

The summer of 1918 saw the start of a terrible civil war in Russia. On one side were the Reds – the Communists. On the other side were the Whites – the opponents of the new communist government. Both sides produced propaganda posters like these in order to win support.

1 Read carefully through the sentences you wrote in Steps 1, 2, 3, 4 and 5. Underline all the points which you think could be used effectively in a propaganda poster for your side.

2 Choose your best idea and write detailed notes to help an illustrator design your propaganda poster for you.

Red and White propaganda posters

Ireland divided

How can people interpret history so differently?

In 1996 a new film was released. Like many other films it took a story from history and tried to bring it to life. In this case the story was set in Ireland between 1916 and 1922. At that time the whole of Ireland was still part of the British Empire. But many of the Irish were **nationalists**: they wanted a separate Irish nation to be ruled by the Irish people – and they were prepared to use violence to break away from British control. At the centre of the violence – and at the centre of the film – was one of the nationalists' most remarkable leaders: Michael Collins.

Think

● What sort of man do you think Michael Collins was according to this film poster?

A poster advertising the film, 'Michael Collins', 1996

Michael Collins

A GEFFEN PICTURES RELEASE

As soon as it was shown, people began to criticise the film director.

He has changed the facts!

He's left out some really important bits!

He's turned it into a love story!

It makes Collins seem heroic – but he's a killer.

He's ignored other important leaders.

Shh! Don't get so worked up about it – it's only a film.

It is not only films which make people argue about history. Any attempt to explain the past can cause disagreements. This is because so many things in history are matters of opinion. Whenever we think about the past and try to describe or explain it to other people we are creating an **interpretation** which others may disagree with. Interpretations take many forms such as:

- museum displays
- university lectures
- advertisements
- historical novels
- television programmes
- textbooks… such as this one!

Think

- How might a film director alter a film to keep the audience or producers happy?

- Since this film came out, historians have found important new documents about Michael Collins. What does this tell you about another difficulty for the film maker?

- Does it matter if a film about someone in history is not strictly accurate and fair?

Your enquiry

Michael Collins

Some people call Michael Collins a heroic leader. Some call him a brutal murderer. Interpretations vary. In this enquiry you will follow his life story through the violent years which led to Ireland being split into two nations. The causes of the split are so complicated that you will not be able to make your own, fair interpretation of why Ireland was divided by the end of this enquiry. But you will be able to show why it is so difficult to make fair interpretations of history.

Early years

Michael Collins was born in 1890 when the whole of Ireland was still ruled by the British government in London. Collins lived near Cork in the south of Ireland. His childhood affected his whole view of life.

When Collins was born his father was 75 years old! He told Michael many stories passed down from his ancestors. He told Michael how the Collins family had once been proud landowners before the English destroyed their wealth.

At school Michael was taught by a man with strong views on Irish history. Here are some things he taught Michael:

- The English conquered Ireland in the Middle Ages.

- The Irish stayed loyal to the Roman Catholic Church when the English became Protestant in 1534.

- From the 1590s, Protestants from Scotland and England took over the best Irish land, especially in the north.

- The Irish were crushed by Oliver Cromwell in 1649 and William of Orange in 1690.

- The English had refused to let the Irish have their own parliament ever since 1800.

- Irish MPs in the London parliament were never able to win 'Home Rule' for Ireland.

In later years Collins always said that it was this teacher who made him a nationalist by stirring his love for Ireland and his desire to end English rule.

There were other powerful stories from the past that affected Michael Collins. Most families in Ireland had awful stories to tell of the Great Famine of 1845–51. That was when the potato harvest failed and hundreds of thousands of people died. Most Catholics believed that England did nothing to help. Michael's grandmother told him how bodies lay rotting at the roadsides. Millions of Irish moved to the USA, taking with them their hatred of the English.

Another story that Michael remembered was about the day when the agent of an English landlord came to throw an Irish farmer off his farm for not paying the rent – even though the farmer was dying at the time. One of the farmer's sons put a pitchfork through the eye of the agent. The evictions stopped straight away! Michael always used this story to show that the only way to get the English to treat Ireland fairly was to use violence.

Think

- How far should the teaching of history in schools encourage patriotism (a love of your country)?

- How has your own childhood affected your view of history? Think about where you were born and stories you have been told.

Even Michael's hobbies filled his mind with a love for Ireland's past and a sense of how her freedom had been taken away. He loved to play traditional Irish sports such as Gaelic football and to sing songs about ancient legends in the Gaelic language.

Of course, there was another side to all these stories about the past – but Michael rarely heard the Protestant point of view. If he had been born into a Protestant family in the north he would almost certainly have grown up as a **Unionist**. Almost all Irish Protestants were Unionists. They were the strongest group in the northern part of Ireland. They were proud to be united with Britain.

The Unionists could tell their own stories of times when the Catholics had treated Protestants dreadfully and how nationalists had invited foreign enemies to use Ireland as a base for attacking England.

But Michael was a Catholic from the south and the Irish Catholic view of history shaped his whole life.

A photograph of a County Cork landscape

Think

● What is the difference between a Nationalist and a Unionist?

● Would someone writing a biography of Michael Collins have to write about the Protestant point of view on all these events even if Michael Collins did not know about them?

STEP 1

Copy the table below. In each column list some examples similar to the ones shown. Find your ideas from pages 42 to 45.

Different ways of passing on interpretations of history	Why interpretations can be misleading
Stories told to children	Children may believe everything they are told

The Easter Rising

By 1914 Irish Members of Parliament (MPs) had persuaded the British government to grant **Home Rule** to Ireland. This meant that Ireland would have its own parliament in Dublin, but the MPs there would still have to swear loyalty to the British king. However, when the First World War started, Home Rule was delayed.

In the early years of the war, thousands of Protestant and Catholic Irishmen volunteered to fight for Britain. Others – like Michael Collins – thought that this was a ridiculous idea.

Think

● What is the difference between Home Rule for Ireland and an Irish republic?

By this time Collins wanted more than Home Rule for Ireland. He wanted an Irish **republic** which was completely free from British control.

At Easter 1916 Collins took part in an event which many now remember as a turning point in the history of Ireland. A small group of extreme nationalists captured some important buildings in Dublin. They declared that they had set up a new Irish Republic. Dubliners were astonished. Hardly any of them supported the rising. After five days the British army regained control by bombarding the rebels with artillery fire and rounding them up.

Think

● This magazine was published soon after the Easter Rising. How does it make the rebellion seem dramatic?

● Why do you think the magazine used such a dramatic illustration on its cover?

At first almost everyone agreed that the rebels were mad to fight for a republic. As Collins and the other captives were led away crowds of local people jeered and mocked them. But Patrick Pearse, one of the leaders, told a friend, 'After a few years they will see the meaning of what we tried to do,' and he wrote to his mother that 'we shall be blessed by unborn generations'.

Four days after the rising ended the executions began. Over a period of several days British firing squads shot Pearse and thirteen other rebels, including James Connolly who had been wounded and who had to be propped up in a chair as a target. As news of these shocking executions emerged, the mood of many Irish people changed.

This popular song was written about a year after the rising. It shows how people in the south of Ireland were interpreting the Easter Rising by that time:

As more people turned against Britain fewer nationalist Irishmen volunteered to join the army to fight against the Germans. This angered Unionist families in the north whose sons were still volunteering to fight and were dying on the battlefields of France. Early in 1918 the British government passed a **conscription** law. This allowed the British to force Irishmen to join the British army. The government never actually used the conscription law but it turned many more Irish people against the British and made them sympathise with the Easter Rising rebels.

Think

- What was conscription?

- Why do you think Irish nationalists were angry that the British government might conscript them?

- How were Irish opinions about the Easter Rising changing?

Let Erin [Ireland] remember Easter Week

and her faithful sons who saved her

With pride in our voice their names

we speak

and scorn for the ruthless invader.

Pearse was right. As time passed many people changed their minds about the Easter Rising. The rebels who had once been jeered and mocked became national heroes. Years later, the south of Ireland finally won the right to exist as a separate nation. Its government then interpreted the Easter Rising as a great success.

The government named important streets in Dublin after rebels who died. It also set up this statue in the post office where Pearse had declared Ireland to be a republic in 1916. Some words from his declaration are shown under the statue. The statue itself shows Cu Chulainn, a legendary Irish warrior who was famous as the defender of Ireland long before the English took over.

Of course, Unionists do not interpret the rebels as heroes. Unionist historians prefer to remind readers of the first reactions to the Easter Rising. One called it:

> The most unpopular rebellion that has ever been made in Ireland.

From S. Ervine 'Craigavon', 1949

Think

● How has the Irish government shown that it is proud of the Easter Rising?

STEP 2

Use information from the section called 'The Easter Rising' to add more ideas to the two lists you started in Step 1.

The war of independence

Collins spent eight months in prison for his small part in the Easter Rising. On his release he joined the **Sinn Fein party**. Sinn Fein said Home Rule for Ireland was not enough: it wanted an Irish republic. More and more Irish people agreed as these 1918 general election results show:

	Before 1918 election	After 1918 election
Sinn Fein MPs	7	73
Home Rule MPs	78	6
Unionist MPs	18	26

The Sinn Fein MPs refused to go to London to sit in parliament there. Instead they set up their own parliament in Dublin. They called it the Dail. The leader of the Dail was Eamon de Valera.

De Valera put Collins in charge of finance and of the spying system. Collins also built up the Irish Republican Army (IRA). This was a force of volunteers who were prepared to fight for the new republic in Ireland.

Eamon de Valera

When the First World War ended the British **Prime Minister**, David Lloyd George, told everyone at the Paris peace conference that new, self-governing nations must be set up all over Europe. Perhaps he would now let the Irish rule themselves? He did not.

The British banned all republican newspapers and speakers and arrested de Valera and other Sinn Fein leaders. Collins escaped. Over the next two years he:

- organised ruthless IRA murder squads
- developed a new kind of warfare using secret, sudden murders and bombings
- inspired others to fight for freedom from British control
- built up a network of spies, including some who worked inside the British headquarters
- risked his life to take messages between IRA agents, cycling through the streets of Dublin under the noses of the British
- ordered the deaths of many British government officials and Irish policemen.

Soon after Collins died, the civil war ended. In 1932 de Valera became the leader of the Irish Free State. He quickly set about breaking ties with Britain. In 1949 the Free State declared complete independence and became the Irish Republic.

Meanwhile, Northern Ireland stayed united with Britain because the Unionists controlled the parliament there. But there were many Catholics in the north as well. They noticed that the Protestant Unionists generally had the best jobs and the best houses.

Most Catholics felt they were being treated badly. Many still wanted a single Irish nation to be ruled from Dublin.

By 1970 extreme nationalists and Unionists in Northern Ireland were turning on each other with guns and bombs. In cities such as Belfast, some Unionists and nationalists decorated their houses with wall paintings.

These show the different interpretations of history that divided them.

A Unionist mural in Belfast

KING WILLIAM III.

JULY   1690

A Nationalist mural in Belfast

Think

- To which events mentioned on page 44 do these two murals refer?

In the late 1990s, Ireland made moves towards peace. If the peace holds it will be a sign that the different groups no longer allow their different interpretations of history to drive them apart.

STEP 4

Use the information from the section called 'The death warrant' to add more ideas to the two lists that you started in Step 1.

Thinking your enquiry through

Use the ideas from the two lists you made in Steps 1, 2, 3 and 4 to write an essay. The title is 'Why people interpret history differently'.

Here are opening lines for four paragraphs. You can use these to get started or you can plan your own approach.

When we talk about an interpretation of history, we mean...

We get our interpretations of history in many different ways. For example...

Interpretations of history can be misleading. There are several reasons for this...

It is important to think carefully about interpretations of history because...

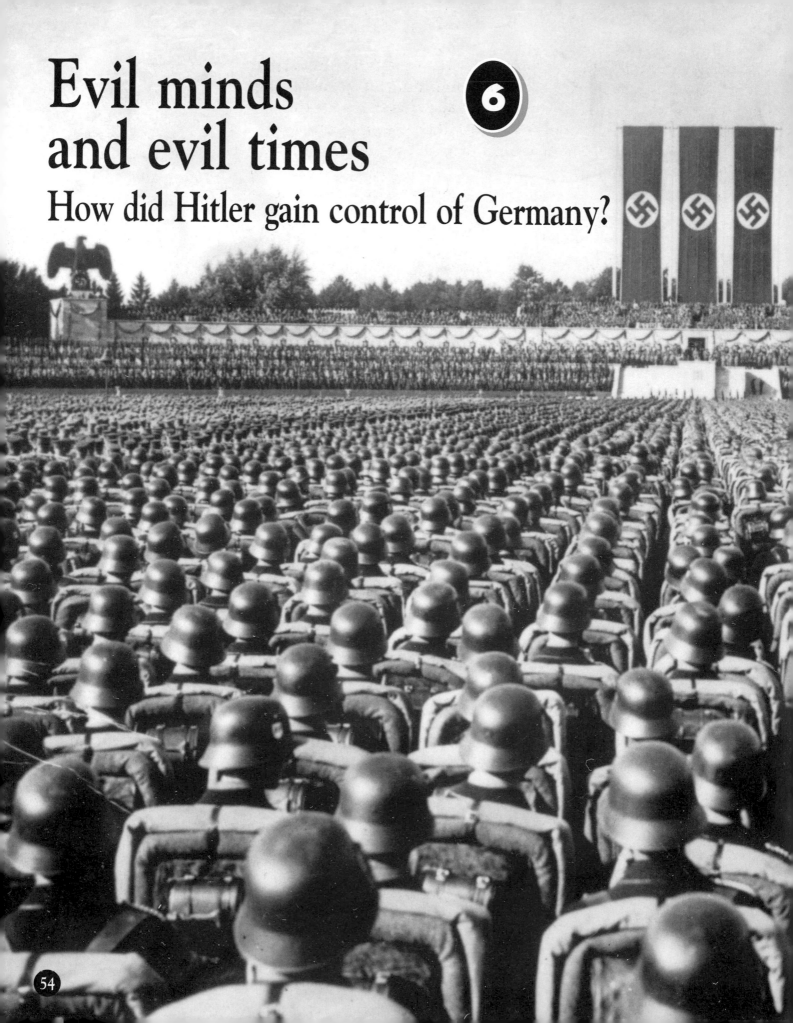

Evil minds and evil times

How did Hitler gain control of Germany?

6

The photograph on the opposite page was taken in Germany in 1938. For one week each September thousands of German people packed into the city of Nuremberg. They were there for the Nuremberg rally. In the huge stadium they watched line after line of soldiers marching in perfect order. They listened to the music of the massed bands. They admired the flying displays of the German air force. Above all, they wanted to hear their leader

– Adolf Hitler.

Hitler was a **dictator**. He ruled Germany alone without consulting a parliament or the German people. During the 1930s Hitler's **Nazi party** gained more and more support. By 1938 the Nazis controlled almost every aspect of life in Germany. The Gestapo – the Nazi secret police – had spies everywhere. Anyone who dared to criticise Hitler or the Nazis could be arrested and placed in a **concentration camp**.

Your enquiry

In this enquiry you will find out how Hitler became Germany's dictator in the years between 1918 and 1938. In order to explain your ideas you will plan a series of three new television programmes. Your programmes will cover the **most important events** and will explain the **most important factors** which helped Hitler gain control of Germany.

Think

● How does the photograph of the Nuremberg rally show Hitler's power?

A painting of Adolf Hitler, 1940

Beginnings, 1918–24

Adolf Hitler was born in Austria in 1889. His father was a violent drunk who made Hitler's childhood very unhappy. At the age of eighteen Hitler ran away to the Austrian capital, Vienna. He hoped to become an art student, but he had little talent and failed to get a place at college. In Vienna he started to live rough, doing odd jobs to survive and living little better than a tramp. Hitler was a failure, a loner, a loser.

All this changed with the First World War. Hitler volunteered to fight in the German army. He was a brave soldier and was quickly promoted to lance-corporal. Towards the end of the war Hitler was blinded in a British gas attack. When the war ended in November 1918 he was still in hospital recovering from the injury to his eyes. Hitler later said that the war was 'the greatest of all experiences'.

A photograph of Hitler (right) and comrades during the First World War

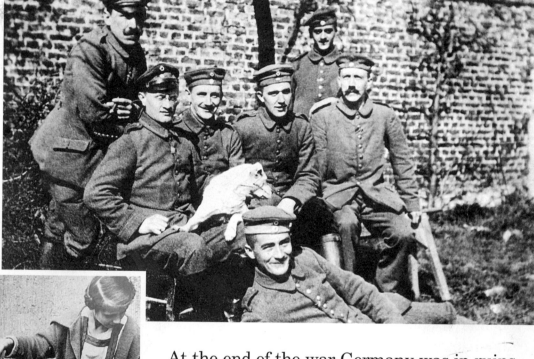

A photograph of children in Germany using worthless banknotes as toys, 1923

At the end of the war Germany was in ruins. Kaiser Wilhelm fled to the Netherlands leaving a new, **democratic** government to try to pick up the pieces. There was bitterness and anger in Germany at the terms of the Treaty of Versailles. Many German people criticised their new leaders for signing it. Things became even worse after 1923 when huge price rises led to unemployment and hunger for millions of German people. Soon the German **currency** became almost worthless. People needed a barrowful of notes to buy a loaf of bread. Children used banknotes as toys.

When the First World War ended, Hitler went to live in Munich. It was there that he became involved in politics. By 1922 Hitler was the leader of a tiny political party – the Nazis. His brilliant speeches soon gained him a lot of support. Hitler organised the Nazi party along military lines. He formed his own private army known as Storm-troopers. It was their job to beat up and terrorise opponents.

A photograph of Nazi 'Storm-troopers', 1933

In 1923 Hitler made his first clumsy grab for power. He planned to march into Berlin with his Storm-troopers and to remove the Weimar government from power. This was known as the Beer Hall Putsch as it started in a Munich pub. The uprising was an embarrassing failure. Sixteen Nazis were killed and Hitler himself was arrested and sent to prison. It was in prison, in 1924, that Hitler started writing his book *Mein Kampf* which means 'my struggle'. Here are some of the most important points which Hitler made in *Mein Kampf*:

- Germany needs a strong government led by a single leader.
- Germany demands land and **colonies** to feed our people.
- The Germans are the master-race. They must keep themselves pure.
- No Jews may be members of the nation. They helped to bring about Germany's defeat in the First World War. They must be destroyed.

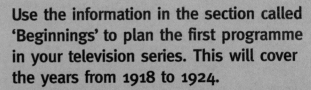

STEP 1

Use the information in the section called 'Beginnings' to plan the first programme in your television series. This will cover the years from 1918 to 1924.

1 Make a timeline to show the **main events** which you will include in your programme.

2 Write down the three **most important factors** which helped Hitler during these years.

Hitler's rise to power, 1924–34

Hitler was released from prison in 1924. For the next five years the Nazi party failed to gain much further support in Germany. In 1929 things changed dramatically. A world **economic depression** hit Germany hard. All kinds of Germans suffered hardship. Workers lost their jobs, the middle classes lost their savings, wealthy industrialists saw their businesses threatened. To all these people Hitler made great promises: he offered **easy solutions to difficult problems**.

This graph shows you what happened to people's jobs and to Hitler's popularity.

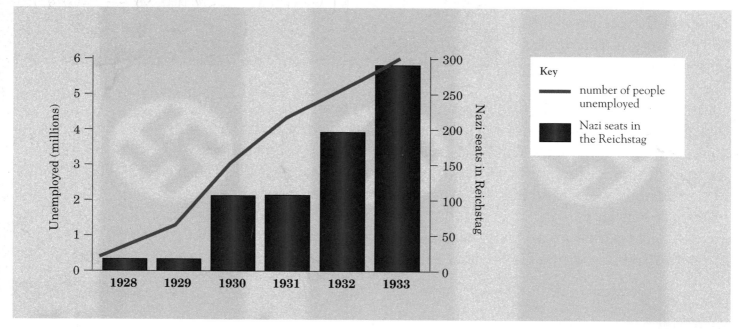

Unemployment and Nazi seats in the Reichstag, 1928–33

By 1932 German voters had made Hitler's Nazis the largest single party. In January 1933 the elderly President Hindenburg asked Hitler to become Chancellor of Germany. Hindenburg thought that Hitler might solve Germany's economic problems. He also thought that Hitler would be easy to control. This was a terrible mistake!

Hitler now took his big chance. In February 1933 Germany's Reichstag (parliament) building was burnt to the ground. A young Dutch **communist** was found near the scene of the crime and was arrested. But some historians think that he was framed and that it was Hitler who was behind what had happened. Hitler now used the Reichstag fire as an excuse to arrest many of his communist opponents.

With the opposition out of the way Hitler could do as he pleased. In March 1933 the Enabling Act was passed. This gave Hitler the power to pass any new laws that he wanted. But Hitler did not stop there. He now turned on those people within his own party whom he did not trust.

On the night of 30 June 1934 Hitler's own personal bodyguards – the SS – were sent out to murder leading members of the Nazi party who opposed Hitler. This later became known as the Night of the Long Knives.

The next day the SS continued to shoot people on their doorsteps. Meanwhile Hitler gave a tea party in his garden.

On 2 August 1934, only one month after the Night of the Long Knives, President Hindenburg died. Within an hour it was announced that Hitler was now not only Chancellor, but also Head of State and Commander of the Army. Hitler was now in complete control of Germany. He was a **dictator**.

A photograph of the Reichstag fire, 1933

STEP 2

Use the information in the section called 'Hitler's rise to power, 1924–34' to plan the second programme in your television series. This will cover the years from 1924 to 1934.

1 Make a timeline to show the **main events** which you will include in your programme.

2 Write down the three **most important factors** which helped Hitler during these years.

Hitler in control, 1934–38

Hitler was now 'Führer' – leader of Germany. But not everyone supported Hitler and the Nazis in 1934. It was now important to create a **one-party state** in which everyone showed complete obedience to their leader. Hitler achieved this using four main methods.

Method 1 – Terror

Hitler's main weapon against his opponents was the SS. After 1934 the SS grew into a huge organisation. Its main task was to terrorise German people into obedience. SS officers arrested people and imprisoned them without trial.

Jews, communists and others who were brave enough to oppose the Nazis were taken to concentration camps. In these isolated prisons people were tortured and forced to do hard labour.

Deaths in the concentration camps became more and more common.

The force which ordinary German people feared most was the Gestapo – Hitler's secret police. The Gestapo tapped telephones and spied on people. Anyone who criticised Hitler was in danger of arrest. The Gestapo had a network of informers across Germany. People lived in fear of their neighbours. The eyes and ears of the Gestapo were everywhere.

A photograph of the Gestapo arresting Jews, 1942

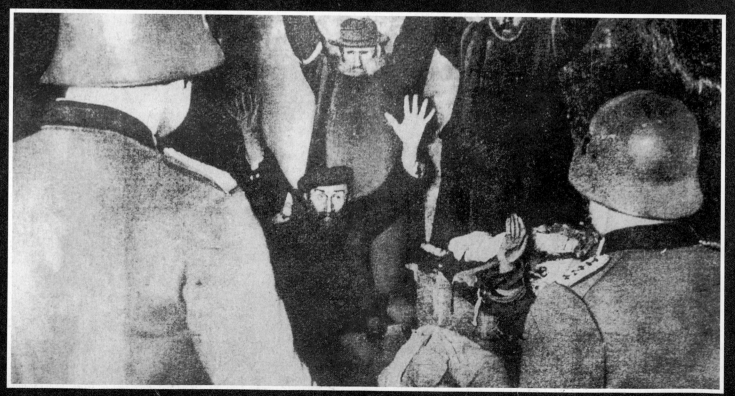

Method 2 – Propaganda

If Hitler was to force the German people into obedience he knew that he must gain control of their minds. In order to do this Hitler appointed Joseph Goebbels as Minister for Propaganda. Goebbels introduced strict controls over what the German people read, heard and saw:

- No books were to be published without Goebbels's permission.
- Anti-Nazi newspapers were closed down.
- Only films carrying the Nazi message were shown in the cinemas.
- No one was allowed to listen to foreign radio stations.
- The Nazis displayed posters all over Germany showing how great they were and attacking their enemies.
- Rallies and parades were organised to show the strength of the Nazi party.

A Nazi propaganda poster
The words mean 'VICTORY WILL BE OURS!'

61

Method 3 – Youth

Hitler knew that it was important for Germany's young people to be loyal Nazis. At school, history lessons concentrated on the rise of the Nazis and the evils of communism. In biology pupils learned how the Germanic people, known as Aryans, were superior to other races. Teachers who did not support Nazi ideas were sacked.

From 1936 all young people had to belong to the Hitler Youth. On the surface this was like the Scouts or Guides. Teenagers marched in parades and played in bands. They went to camps where they played sports, worked on farms and sang songs around the camp fire. Germany's young people were made to feel that they were part of a great nation again.

But underneath something more sinister was happening. Boys were being trained for obedient service and loyalty in the armed forces. Girls were being prepared for their role as perfect German mothers of perfect German children.

A photograph of members of the Hitler Youth in the 1930s

Method 4 – Economic success

Before 1933 most working-class people in Germany did not support the Nazis. Hitler knew that he needed to control these people, especially the six million ordinary Germans who were unemployed. After 1934 he created a number of schemes to provide work. New roads and buildings were constructed all over Germany. More and more people were given jobs in the armed forces. Many workers were grateful to Hitler for providing them with work.

Workers were not allowed to strike. However, Nazi Germany gave its workers many benefits. A scheme known as Strength through Joy was set up to organise the leisure time of the workers. They went on cut-price holidays and started to save up for one of the new Volkswagen Beetles which Hitler called the People's Car. To these people it seemed as if Germany had entered a time of peace and plenty – but we now know that war was just around the corner.

A photograph of a Volkswagen Beetle, 1938

STEP 3

You now need to plan the final programme in your television series. This will cover the years from 1934 to 1938. Your final programme will focus on three individuals who gave their support to Hitler during these years. Use the information in the section called 'Hitler in control, 1934–38' to list as many reasons as you can why each of these people might have supported the Nazis:

- a factory worker who had no job in 1933
- a teenage boy who joined the Hitler Youth in 1936
- a housewife who joined the Nazi party even though she did not agree with all their ideas.

Thinking your enquiry through

You need to complete the plans for your television series by deciding on a title for the series and by writing the voice-over for a trailer advertising the new series. Use the information from the Steps to explain your ideas about how Hitler gained control of Germany.

The road to war

What caused the Second World War?

On 31 August 1939 Hitler sent this document to the leading generals of the German army. It was an order to invade Poland.

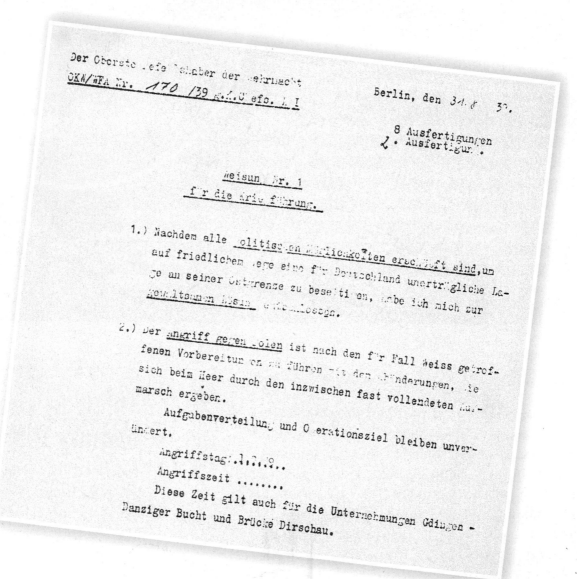

The next day, 1 September 1939, German tanks forced their way across the Polish border. Two days later Poland's allies, Britain and France, declared war on Germany. **The most terrible war in the history of the world had begun.**

Your enquiry

Historians disagree about the causes of the Second World War. Many historians think that Hitler had a plan to dominate the world. They argue that Hitler's order to invade Poland was part of that plan. Other historians feel that Hitler had no clear plan. They claim that politicians from other countries should accept some responsibility for the war. In this enquiry you will find out about the events leading up to 1939 and will make up your own mind about the causes of the Second World War.

A photograph of Nazi troops invading Poland, September 1939

Hitler's war

Hitler's words

Before he rose to power, Hitler set out his vision for the future of Germany in his book *Mein Kampf*. Many historians believe that the ideas in Hitler's book provided a plan for the things he did in the 1930s. Here are some points from *Mein Kampf*:

- The Treaty of Versailles must be cancelled and land taken from Germany must be returned.
- All people of German blood (including many in Austria and Czechoslovakia) must be allowed to live in Greater Germany.
- We demand living space ('Lebensraum') for our people in the east.
- The Germans are the 'Master Race'.

Think

- Why might some of the things which Hitler wrote in *Mein Kampf* lead to another war in Europe?

Hitler's actions

1933

Within days of becoming leader Hitler began to build up Germany's armed forces. At first this was done in secret, but from 1935 the Nazis no longer tried to hide their plans for re-armament. German re-armament was against the terms of the Treaty of Versailles, but Hitler chose to ignore the Treaty.

1936

Hitler introduced **conscription**. Every German man now had to spend some time in the army, navy or air force.

A photograph of German soldiers and weapons on show in Berlin, 1935

A photograph of German troops re-occupying the Rhineland, 1936

In March German troops were sent to re-occupy the Rhineland. The Treaty of Versailles had not allowed any German forces into this area in order to give France a **buffer** against another invasion. Once again Hitler chose to ignore the Treaty.

1937

Hitler helped the Spanish **dictator**, Franco, to win the civil war in Spain. Some historians think that Hitler used the Spanish Civil War to test out his new weapons and aircraft.

March 1938

Hitler demanded that Austria should be joined with Germany. This was forbidden by the Treaty of Versailles, but Hitler ignored the Treaty. German troops entered Austria unchallenged.

September 1938

Hitler declared that he was prepared to occupy the Sudetenland, a part of Czecho-slovakia, order to protect the German-speaking people living there. Britain and France agreed that Germany could take over the Sudetenland as long as Hitler promised not to invade the rest of Czechoslovakia. This was known as the Munich agreement.

March 1939

Hitler ignored the Munich agreement by invading the rest of Czechoslovakia.

September 1939

Hitler demanded that Poland return the Polish Corridor and the port of Danzig to Germany. He claimed that this land should not have been taken away from Germany by the Treaty of Versailles. **On 1 September German troops invaded Poland.**

A map of central Europe in 1939

STEP 1

1 Use the information in the section called 'Hitler's war' to make a set of Explanation Cards to show how Hitler's words and actions led to war in 1939. An Explanation Card might say:

> ### Explanation Card
> Hitler ignored the Treaty of Versailles and began to re-arm Germany. This gave him a big enough army to go to war.

2 Decide whether you think the idea or action on each Explanation Card was quite important or very important in causing the Second World War. Mark each of your cards QI (Quite Important) or VI (Very Important).

Appeasement

Explaining the causes of the Second World War is not as simple as just blaming Hitler. If the leaders of other powerful countries had stopped Hitler sooner, perhaps the war could have been avoided. Other countries, like Britain and France, did little to stand up to Hitler during the 1930s. Some historians argue that these countries must share part of the blame for the start of the war.

In 1938 Britain had a new and popular **Prime Minister** – Neville Chamberlain. Chamberlain had lived through the horrors of the First World War and he was determined to do everything he could to stop another one. This is what he said in 1938:

> When I think of those four terrible years of the First World War, and I think of the seven million young men who were killed, the thirteen million who were maimed and mutilated, I feel it is my duty to strain every nerve to avoid a repetition of the First World War.

Chamberlain believed that the best way to avoid another war was to follow a **policy** of **appeasement** towards Hitler. If you appease someone you decide to give them most of what they want to keep them happy. You hope that they will be satisfied and will stop making even more demands. This was exactly the way that Chamberlain thought he could deal with Hitler's demands over Czechoslovakia in 1938. When Hitler demanded the Sudetenland it looked like a war was bound to start. But in September Chamberlain arranged a last-minute meeting with Hitler in Munich.

Everyone held their breath.

At the end of the meeting the two leaders signed the famous Munich agreement. This stated that Germany could have the Sudetenland as long as Hitler would stop demanding more territory. Chamberlain returned to a hero's welcome in London. He waved a paper containing Hitler's signature. Chamberlain believed that this guaranteed 'peace in our time'.

A photograph of Chamberlain on his return from Munich, 1938

This is how one British newspaper cartoonist showed what Chamberlain was trying to achieve.

Chamberlain did not succeed in guiding the world into peace. In March 1939 Nazi troops invaded the rest of Czechoslovakia. Britain and France did nothing. Hitler was encouraged by the fact that he had been allowed to get away with things once again. He now sent his troops into Poland. This time Britain and France declared war on Germany.

Appeasement failed, but historians still argue about whether Chamberlain was right to have tried this policy at the time. This is what some historians have said about appeasement:

- Appeasement was a major mistake. It gave Hitler the idea that he could continue to do as he liked in Europe.
- Appeasement gave Hitler an important advantage. He had more time to re-arm before invading Poland.
- Appeasement was necessary as Britain needed time to re-arm and be ready for a full-scale war.
- Appeasement was popular as many people in Britain were more scared of the spread of **communism** than they were of the Nazis. A strong Germany was a barrier against the expansion of the Soviet Union.
- Appeasement was a reasonable policy as the Treaty of Versailles had been very harsh on Germany by taking away land and resources.

Think

- What does the cartoon show?
- Why do you think that the cartoonist chose to draw Chamberlain in this way?

STEP 2

1 Use the information in the section called 'Appeasement' to make just one explanation card, by copying and completing these statements.

Appeasement means…

Chamberlain tried to appease Hitler because…

Some historians believe that appeasement helped to cause the war. They say…

Other factors leading to war

So far we have looked at two main causes of the Second World War:

1 Hitler's plan and his actions after 1933

2 The policy of appeasement which encouraged Hitler.

Some historians think that we need to dig deeper than this.
They think that other factors were also important in explaining
the outbreak of war in 1939.

Factor 1: The Treaty of Versailles

After 1919 many German people were angry and resentful about the Treaty of Versailles. Germany had lost 10% of her land and all of her overseas **colonies**. Her army was limited to 100,000 men and she could have only a tiny navy and no air force. Worst of all, Germany had to accept all the blame for starting the war and had to pay huge **reparations**. In 1923 Germany could no longer afford to pay. The French invaded part of Germany called the Ruhr to take industrial goods instead of reparations. All of these problems made the German people more willing to listen to Hitler's extreme ideas about how to win back Germany's power and prestige.

Think

- How has the cartoonist suggested that Germany faced problems after the Treaty of Versailles?

A cartoon by Wilhelm Schulz from 'Simplicissimus', 1919

Factor 2: The failure of the League of Nations

The Treaty of Versailles set up an international organisation called the League of Nations. This was supposed to stop any wars from ever happening again. However, during the 1930s the League of Nations was not strong enough to stand up to dictators like Hitler.

In particular it failed to do anything in 1935 when the Italian dictator, Mussolini, invaded Abyssinia. Some historians think that because Hitler saw Mussolini getting away with aggression in Africa he may have been encouraged to do the same in Europe.

Think

● What does this cartoon suggest about the power of the League of Nations?

A cartoon from the magazine 'Punch', 1920

Factor 3: The American policy of isolationism

The League of Nations was the brainchild of the American **President**, Woodrow Wilson. However, the USA eventually refused to join the League. This was because other American politicians believed that one European war had already cost too many young American lives. During the 1920s and 1930s the USA therefore followed a policy called **isolationism**. The USA chose to ignore events in Europe. Because of this policy, Hitler knew that the only country strong enough to stop him simply would not do anything.

THE GAP IN THE BRIDGE.

A cartoon from the magazine 'Punch', 1919

Think

- What does this cartoonist think about the American decision to stay out of the League of Nations?

Factor 4: The Nazi-Soviet Pact

If the USA helped to cause the Second World War, so too did the Soviet Union. In August 1939 many people in the west were amazed when Hitler and the Russian dictator, Stalin, signed an agreement not to fight each other. Stalin and Hitler hated each other, but each man had his own reasons for wanting to reach an agreement. Stalin thought that Hitler might attack the Soviet Union. If he signed an agreement it would give the Soviet Union more time to prepare for battle. Hitler thought that a temporary peace with the Soviet Union would allow him to fight Britain and France in the west. The Soviet Union could be finished off later!

72

A cartoon published in 1939

Think

- What message does the cartoonist want to give about the Nazi-Soviet Pact?

STEP 3

1 Make an Explanation Card for each of the factors on pages 70–73 to summarise how it led to war in 1939.

2 For each factor decide whether you think the explanation was Quite Important or Very Important in causing the Second World War. Mark each of your cards QI (Quite Important) or VI (Very Important).

Thinking your enquiry through

You are now going to write an essay to answer the question: What caused the Second World War? Here are opening lines for five paragraphs. You can use these to get started or you can plan your own approach. Remember to write in detail about the explanations from your Very Important Explanation Cards.

The Second World War had many causes and historians disagree about which are the most important…

Many historians argue that Hitler's words and actions were definitely to blame for the war…

However, other historians argue that Chamberlain's policy of appeasement was also a major cause of the war…

A range of other factors contributed to the outbreak of war in 1939…

Overall, I think that the most important causes of the Second World War were…

The world dissolved in flames

8

How did the Allies win the Second World War?

This photograph shows the German city of Dresden in 1945. On 13–14 February British and American aircraft bombed Dresden so heavily that they caused a huge firestorm. At least 35,000 people were killed. Hurricane winds sucked people into the intense heat. In seconds they were burnt to cinders. Men, women and children were fried alive on the melting roads.

The Second World War was a Total War. Air raids like the one on Dresden meant that **civilians** as well as soldiers perished. As this map shows, fighting took place on every continent except the Americas. During the six long years between 1939 and 1945, fifty million people lost their lives. The Second World War was the largest and most terrifying conflict the world had ever seen.

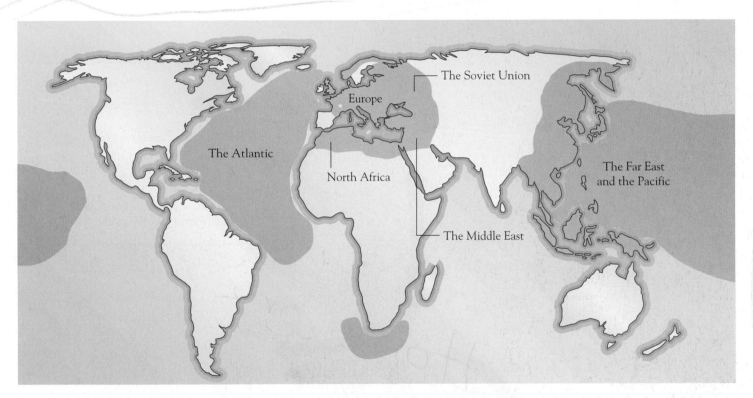

The Soviet Union

Europe

The Atlantic

North Africa

The Far East and the Pacific

The Middle East

Where the main fighting took place in the Second World War

Your enquiry

On 8 May 1945, less than three months after the bombing of Dresden, Germany surrendered. In August 1945, after the dropping of atomic bombs on Hiroshima and Nagasaki, Japan also surrendered. The Second World War was over. The Allies (Britain, the Soviet Union, the USA and a host of other countries) had finally defeated the Axis powers (Germany, Italy and Japan). In this enquiry you will find out about the main events of the war. At the end of the enquiry you will produce a wallchart to explain how the Allies won the Second World War.

Dark days

The war started in September 1939. **Nazi** aeroplanes and tanks ripped through Poland in a Blitzkrieg (lightning war). Poland was quickly defeated by the Nazis, but in the west the war developed quite slowly. In fact, because there was no real fighting, people in Britain called it the Phoney War. But things soon changed. In the spring of 1940 the war started to go very well for the Nazis. During February and March they quickly occupied the whole of Denmark and Norway. In May Holland, Belgium, Luxembourg and France were occupied as well.

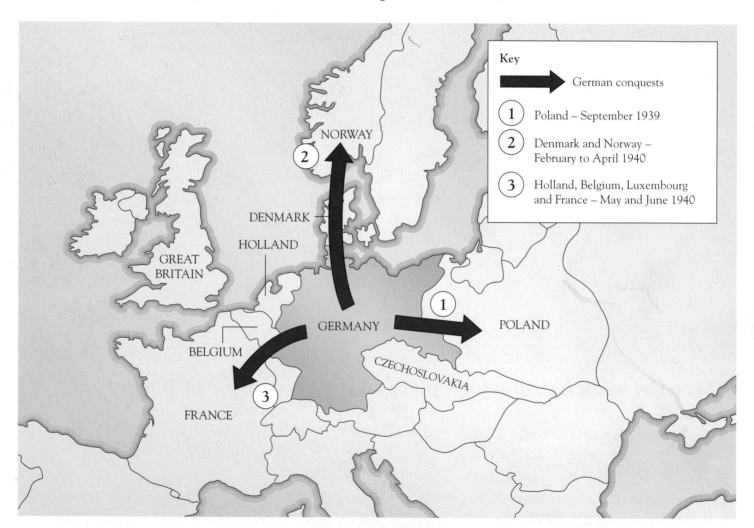

The German advance at the beginning of the war in Europe

The British army in France was almost cut off and nearly captured. At the end of May 1940 it was lucky to escape across the Channel after a speedy **evacuation** from Dunkirk. France itself was not so lucky. In June 1940 France surrendered to the Nazis.

A painting of the evacuation of Dunkirk by Charles Cundall, who was sent by the British government to paint the scene, 1940

Hitler now hoped that he could persuade Britain to agree a peace. He was disappointed. The British **Prime Minister**, Winston Churchill, made it clear that he was not willing to negotiate. Hitler then tried to complete his conquest of western Europe by invading Britain. The first step was to control the air. From July to October 1940 the Royal Air Force and the German Luftwaffe fought the Battle of Britain high in the skies above south east England. This was Britain's first victory in the war. **Propaganda** posters made at the time show how important this was to the British.

"NEVER WAS SO MUCH OWED BY SO MANY TO SO FEW"

THE PRIME MINISTER

A propaganda poster for the Battle of Britain

Think

- Why was the spring of 1940 such a good time for the Nazis?

Think

- Why do you think that the Battle of Britain was such an important event in the war?

A photograph of a scene from the Blitz, 1940

Hitler was forced to give up his plan to invade Britain for the time being. Instead he ordered night bombing raids on British cities. This became known as the Blitz. From September to December 1940 one-and-a-half million homes were damaged in the air raids on London. Over 10,000 men, women and children were killed.

In June 1941 Hitler took a very important decision. He decided to break the Nazi-Soviet Pact. By this agreement of 1939 Germany had promised not to go to war with the Soviet Union. Now he broke that promise. He ordered his troops to invade. It turned out to be a major mistake. Hitler needed to beat the Soviet Union very quickly if the gamble was to work. But the Soviet people defended their country with amazing bravery. As the Soviet army retreated it destroyed anything which might be of use to the Germans. By December 1941 the bitterly cold Russian winter set in. Nazi equipment froze solid. The German army was forced to retreat leaving behind thousands of soldiers who had frozen to death.

A photograph of dead German soldiers in the Soviet Union, December 1941

At the same time as the tide turned against the German army in Russia another important event occurred on the other side of the world. On 7 December 1941 Germany's ally Japan launched a surprise air attack on the American naval base at Pearl Harbor. The Japanese hoped that this would give them complete control of the Pacific. The following day the USA declared war on Japan. From December 1941 Britain and the Soviet Union had a new and powerful ally.

An early colour photograph of the Japanese attack on Pearl Harbor, December 1941

STEP 1

1 Make a timeline for the first part of the Second World War (September 1939 to December 1941). Use the information in the section called 'Dark days' to mark important events and developments on your timeline. Use one colour for Axis victories and another colour for Allied victories.

2 Historians call really important events 'turning points'. A turning point is a moment in history which leads to important changes. Think carefully about the information on your timeline and highlight any events or developments which you think may have been turning points.

The tide turns

From the beginning of 1942 the early successes of the **Axis powers** gradually stopped. In the scorching desert of **North Africa** two great generals – Montgomery for Britain and Rommel for Germany – fought vicious tank battles. It was a hot and gruelling war. Soldiers on both sides burnt to death in their tanks.

In October 1942 Montgomery's troops, the Desert Rats, reinforced by New Zealand forces, defeated the Nazis at El Alamein. This was the first important victory in the war for Allied troops. The Allied forces went on to drive the enemy out of North Africa. By May 1943, after nearly two years of bitter fighting, the desert war was over. Rommel was beaten. Almost one million German and Italian soldiers had been killed or taken prisoner.

A photograph of General Montgomery in the North African desert

This map shows how, in the summer of 1943, Allied forces went on to attack what Churchill called 'the soft under-belly of Europe'. In July 1943 the Allies invaded Sicily. By September Italy had also surrendered.

Think

● Why was the victory at El Alamein so important?

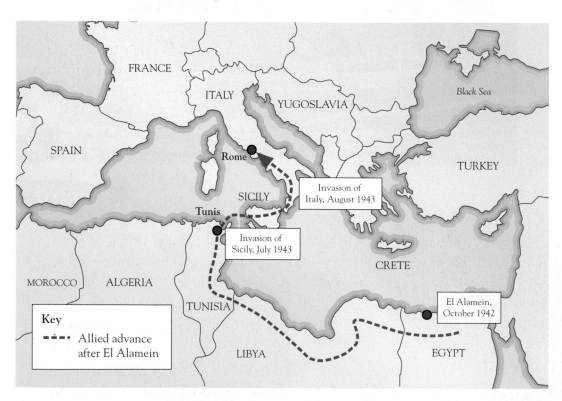

A map showing the Allied advance through North Africa and Italy

1942 was also an important year for the war in the **Far East**. In February the Japanese captured Singapore, but by the summer the tide began to turn. In June 1942 American dive-bombers destroyed Japanese aircraft carriers at the Battle of Midway. The Japanese navy was never again a match for the Americans.

The slow process of re-capturing islands that had been conquered by the Japanese began. It was to take three long years. As American troops moved closer to Japan, more and more soldiers lost their lives. In the attack on the island of Iwo Jima in 1945, 6000 Americans and 21,000 Japanese were killed. The island measured only thirteen square kilometres.

A photograph of the Battle of Stalingrad

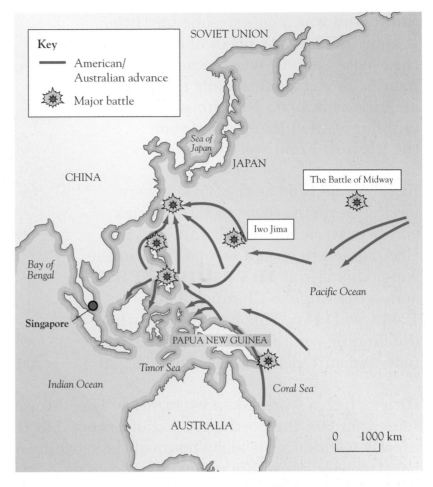

Map of the war in the Far East

Meanwhile, towards the end of 1942 the Soviets began to defeat and then to push back the Nazis on the **Eastern Front**. In a bitterly cold December, the German general, von Paulus, tried to hold on to the city of Stalingrad. Day and night the Russians fought bravely to re-take their city. When the ground froze German tanks could no longer move. Russian forces surrounded von Paulus and his one-and-a-quarter-million men. Hitler ordered his general not to surrender. By February 1943 von Paulus had no choice. By then 70,000 German soldiers had died.

Stalingrad was a catastrophe for Hitler. It ended all Hitler's hopes of conquering the Soviet Union. Over the next few months Soviet armies made a number of quick attacks on Nazi lines. By the autumn of 1943 Hitler's forces on the Eastern Front were defeated.

At the same time as the Soviets were forcing German troops to retreat back across eastern Europe, Britain and the USA agreed to open a second front in the west. This meant **invading France** across the English Channel. 6 June 1944 was D Day. This was the day when the landings on the Normandy beaches, code-named 'Operation Overlord', began.

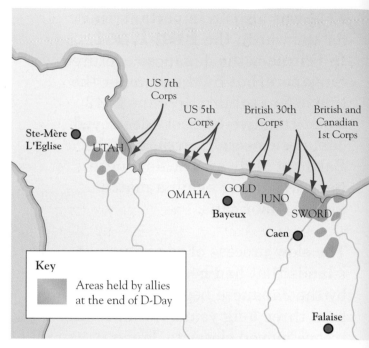

A map of the Normandy landings

Hitler's forces were taken by surprise. They expected an attack somewhere on the northern coast of France, but they did not know exactly where. In the early hours of the morning of 6 June, Allied paratroopers gracefully parachuted down onto French soil. As the day dawned thousands of cold and seasick soldiers stepped onto French sand and walked into the hell of war. The reconquest of Europe had begun.

A photograph of the Normandy landings, 1944

From this point on the Germans faced a war on two fronts – a Soviet advance from the east and a British and American advance through France from the west. At the same time the Royal Air Force stepped up its bombing of German cities. In August 1944 the Allies arrived in Paris. In March 1945 they crossed the Rhine into Germany. In the east the Soviets moved closer and closer towards Berlin. On 30 April Hitler realised that the situation was hopeless and committed suicide. Eight days later, with the Soviets now in Berlin itself, the Germans surrendered. The war in Europe was over.

In the Far East the Second World War dragged on until August 1945. It was not until the cities of Hiroshima and Nagasaki had been destroyed by atomic bombs that the Japanese finally surrendered.

A photograph of Soviet troops arriving in Berlin, 1945

STEP 2

1 Make a timeline for the second part of the Second World War (January 1942 to August 1945). Use the information in the section called 'The tide turns' to mark important events and developments on your timeline. Use one colour for Axis victories and another colour for Allied victories.

2 Think carefully about the information on your timeline and highlight any events or developments which you think may have been turning points.

Thinking your enquiry through

A publishing company has asked you to produce a large illustrated wallchart to explain how the Allies won the Second World War. The wallchart is for primary school children. The publishers do not mind how you set out the wallchart, but they would like you to include the following:

● a timeline showing important turning points

● a world map showing where the war was fought

● illustrations of the three most important events

● some 'in-depth' sections explaining the turning points in greater detail

● a 'summary box' explaining how the Allies won the war.

'The greatest crime in the history of the world'

9

Why is it so important to remember the Holocaust?

A photograph of the entrance to the Auschwitz death camp

Magda Spiegel was sent to Auschwitz during the Second World War. This is what she remembers:

> A few hours after arriving at Auschwitz, I asked some people, 'Where is my little boy?' My son was only seven years old. I was very worried about him.
>
> 'You see those chimneys?' they replied, pointing toward the crematoria. 'Your child is there and, one day, you will also be there.'
>
> The sky was red – red – the whole sky was red!

It was the last year of the transports, and the **Nazis** were putting thousands and thousands of people into the crematoria.

People arrived at Auschwitz in railway trucks. They often travelled huge distances across Europe with no food or water. Many died on the way. When the train reached Auschwitz the people who were well enough were taken off to work as slave labour. The old, the sick and children like Magda Spiegel's son were led straight to the gas chambers. To avoid any panic the Nazis told them that they were going to have a shower. But in the 'shower rooms' they were gassed to death.

Between 1942 and 1944 the Nazis built death camps like Auschwitz all over remote parts of eastern Europe. By 1945 they had killed over six million Jews and hundreds of thousands of others such as gypsies, trade unionists and homosexuals. This mass killing is often referred to as the **Holocaust** which means 'death by fire'. Many Jews prefer to use the term Churban which means 'destruction'.

A recent photograph of ovens used to burn the bodies of the dead at Auschwitz

Your enquiry

Winston Churchill called the Holocaust 'probably the greatest and most horrible single crime ever committed in the history of the world'. In this enquiry you will find out how such a dreadful and disturbing thing could have happened, and think about its importance for us today.

Beginnings

Hatred of Jews is known as anti-Semitism. Historians know that this was not something which suddenly happened in Nazi Germany. Anti-Semitism has been going on for a very long time in many European countries.

In the Middle Ages Jews were often persecuted by Christians who saw them as outcasts. They were often accused of causing disasters like plague. In 1190, 150 Jews were massacred in York. In 1290 all Jews were expelled from England.

In 1543 Martin Luther – the German priest who started the Reformation – wrote a pamphlet called 'On the Jews and Their Lies' which criticised Jewish money-lenders. He wrote that Jewish synagogues should be destroyed.

In the 19th century the country with the largest Jewish population was Russia. When Tsar Alexander II was assassinated in 1881 there were many anti-Jewish riots. Synagogues were burnt down and Jewish people were attacked.

Think

● How does this information help us to explain how the Holocaust could have happened?

Anti-Semitism has a long history, but it got much worse in Germany during the 1930s and 1940s. Hitler had a particularly deep hatred of the Jews. He spent part of his youth in Vienna where anti-Semitism was widespread. Hitler was living little better than a tramp and he grew to hate the rich and successful Jews around him. After the First World War Hitler blamed Jewish business men and bankers for Germany's defeat.

Here are some of the things Hitler said about Jews before he came to power:

The whole of Germany is governed by Jews. The Jew sits in the government and swindles and smuggles. Therefore Germans, be united and fight against the Jews, because they will gobble up our last crumbs.

The aim of Jews is the complete destruction of the German 'Reich' and the spread of revolution.

The bitterest struggle for the victory over Jewry is being waged here in Germany. Here it is the Nazi movement which alone has taken upon itself this struggle against this crime against mankind.

Think

● What kinds of things did Hitler blame the Jews for?

Once in power Hitler and the Nazis started to put their ideas into operation – first in Germany, then in the countries they occupied during the war.

● 1933
Jews were excluded from the civil service and from schools and universities.

● 1935
Nuremberg Laws were passed. Jews could no longer be citizens. Marriage and sexual relations between Jews and Aryans were outlawed.

● 1938
9 November, known as 'Kristallnacht'. Jewish homes, businesses and synagogues were attacked all over Germany. Thousands of Jews fled from the country.

● 1940
When the Nazis conquered Poland they sealed off half a million Jews in part of Warsaw called the Warsaw Ghetto.

● 1941
The Nazi invasion of the USSR brought millions more Jews under Nazi control. Many were shot or placed in ghettos.

● 1942
Leading Nazis decided on the Final Solution to the Jewish problem. Death camps were built.

Think

● How could this gradual build up of persecution explain how the Holocaust happened?

STEP 1

Use the information in the section called 'Beginnings' to write a paragraph explaining how the Holocaust happened.

Reactions
Revolt and resistance

Even though the Nazis were very strong, many people bravely resisted them. As Jews were rounded up all over Europe some people managed to escape. They sometimes formed resistance groups, blowing up railway lines and attacking Nazi soldiers. There were many acts of bravery throughout the war as individuals and groups of people tried to save Jewish lives in Germany and throughout occupied Europe.

A photograph of Jewish resistance fighters being captured, 1943

Think

- There were many acts of resistance during the war. Why do you think they did not stop the Holocaust?

In May 1943 the Jews in the Warsaw Ghetto fought bravely when Nazi troops were sent to destroy the ghetto. Even in the death camps resistance and revolt were not unknown. Jerzy Tabeau, a Polish medical student, managed to escape from Auschwitz.

He reached Hungary where he was able to warn the Hungarian Jews about the atrocities in the death camps. In 1943 a revolt in the death camp of Sosibor was so serious that the Nazis were forced to close the camp and destroy all the buildings.

The Allies

For a while the Nazis tried to keep the Holocaust a secret, but gradually information seeped out. The historian Martin Gilbert tried to find out what the British and American governments knew about Auschwitz. He wrote:

> The British and American governments were receiving information about what was happening at Auschwitz from 1942 onwards. Winston Churchill ordered that a plan be drawn up to see if the gassings could be stopped by bombing the railway lines and gas chambers there. Nothing was done. There were several reasons for this. First, it was argued that bombing Auschwitz could cost the lives of British pilots, even though pilots often flew over Auschwitz on their way to bomb other targets. Secondly, many people could not believe what they heard – it seemed too dreadful to be true. Thirdly, there were many other things that had to be done to win the war at the time, which seemed more important.

Think

- According to Martin Gilbert, why did the British government do nothing about the Holocaust?

Think

- Not all Germans were as anti-Semitic as Hitler. Why do you think so few tried to stop him?

The German people

Although the German media were controlled by Nazis, many Germans probably knew something of what was happening to the Jews. To speak out would have meant imprisonment and probably death. These two extracts also help to explain the reactions of German people. A member of the Hitler Youth recalled how he got to find out about the **extermination** of the Jews:

> I remember being told by a German officer that we were engaged in genocide [the mass killing of a race of people]. First of all I didn't believe him. In fact I was ready to turn him in to the Gestapo. And secondly, it simply didn't sink in, it didn't make any sense. We needed these people for slave labour.

Albert Speer was Hitler's architect and armaments minister. After the war he wrote a book in which he described what he knew about the extermination of the Jews. This is what he said:

> People have often asked me what I knew about the extermination of the Jews. As armaments minister I really only concerned myself with armaments and was isolated from what else was going on. But that is really only an excuse. I did not know exactly what was going on at the camps, but I could have worked it out from the little I did know. I should have done. No apologies are possible.

STEP 2

Use the information in the section called 'Reactions' to write a second paragraph explaining how the Holocaust happened.

Remembering

In 1945 **Allied** troops moved into Germany and eastern Europe and entered the camps. For the Jews in the camps who were still alive the immediate hell was over. It is hard to imagine the feelings of the Jewish survivors in this photograph.

A photograph of the liberation of Auschwitz, 1945

After 1945 the dreadful memory of the Holocaust did not fade in the minds of the survivors. Since the war, attempts have been made to ensure that such mass killings never happen again. Many people still feel that it is important for future generations to remember the Holocaust if people are to live their lives without fear of prejudice and persecution.

In 1948 the United Nations drew up a list of human rights to try to ensure that all people should enjoy freedom from fear. Here are two important Articles from the Universal Declaration of Human Rights:

Article 3
Everyone has the right to life, liberty and security of person.

Article 5
No one shall be subjected to torture or to cruel, inhuman or degrading treatment or punishment.

Despite the Universal Declaration of Human Rights, large-scale persecutions and mass killings still take place.

Much has been done since 1945 to make sure that people do not forget the Holocaust:

- Museums have been set up at the sites of former death camps like Auschwitz and Dachau.

A photograph of Auschwitz today

- Groups like the Spiro Institute work to tell people about the Holocaust.

- Books and films like *The Diary of Anne Frank* or *Schindler's List* help people to understand.

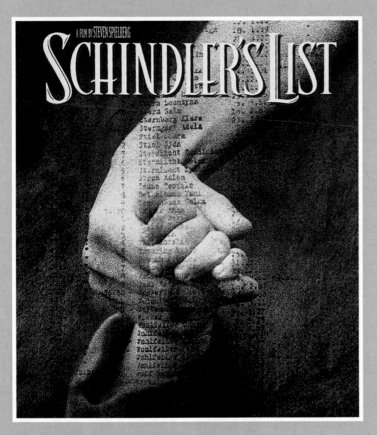

- The Holocaust is studied in classrooms all over the world.

The writer Jonathan Gorsky explains why the Holocaust is still relevant in British schools today:

There are pupils who have become racist through what they have heard on football terraces and read in the press. The brutal power of Nazism will be very like their own impulses and desires. Pupils from ethnic minorities will need little imagination to enter the lives of Jewish children in the Germany of the 1930s.

STEP 3

Use the information in the section called 'Remembering' to write a third paragraph to explain why you think it is important to remember the Holocaust.

Thinking your enquiry through

These people are survivors of the Nazi death camps. Since 1945 they have re-built their lives. They have also worked to ensure that the world does not forget the tragedy of Jewish people during the Second World War.

You should now write a letter to one of the survivors of the Holocaust explaining that you have just studied the Holocaust at school. Use the ideas in your paragraphs to explain:

- what you know and understand about the Holocaust
- how you feel about the Holocaust
- why we should remember the Holocaust.

The bomb that changed the world

10

What were the effects of the atom bombs dropped on Japan?

This picture shows the remains of the Japanese city of Hiroshima a few days after an atomic bomb was dropped on it in August 1945. As the newspaper headline suggests, this was an event that changed the world.

Throughout the Second World War, scientists in America had been working hard to produce an atomic bomb which they believed would be far more powerful than any weapon ever made. The scientists developed the atomic bomb, but the man who had to decide whether to use it was the **President** of the USA, Harry Truman. Truman knew that the bomb would cause massive destruction, but he wanted to end the war with Japan quickly. He gave the order that on August 6th the bomb should be dropped on Hiroshima.

The bomb at Hiroshima killed over 70,000 people immediately. Three days later a second bomb was dropped on Nagasaki. This time 40,000 people died. Many thousands more were to die from injuries and radiation poisoning in the years that followed.

Marcel Junod visited Hiroshima. This is what he wrote about the bombing:

Suddenly a glaring whitish, pinkish light appeared in the sky accompanied by an unnatural tremor which was followed almost immediately by a wave of suffocating heat and a wind which swept everything away in its path.

Within a few seconds the thousands of people in the streets and the gardens were scorched by searing heat. Many were killed instantly, others lay writhing on the ground screaming in agony from the intolerable pain of their burns. Trams were picked up and tossed aside. Trains were flung off the rails as if they were toys. Horses, dogs and cattle suffered the same fate as human beings. Even the vegetation did not escape. Trees went up in flames, the rice plants lost their greenness, the grass burned on the ground like dry straw.

Your enquiry

The dropping of the atomic bombs ended the Second World War. The Japanese surrendered on 14 August 1945. The war was over, but the effects of the atomic bombs have been felt ever since.

Newspapers need a strong sense of history. In this enquiry you will work as a journalist reporting on some of the most significant moments of the nuclear age.

The immediate effects of the bombs

Those who survived the bombing of Hiroshima had alarming stories to tell. One of them, Sawami Katagiri, drew this picture and wrote about it 26 years after the bomb was dropped.

I walked round the city looking for my husband. There were many burned persons at each evacuation centre. I was too shocked to feel loneliness for my husband. This picture shows only a part of Hiroshima. The whole city was just like this at that time.

Think

● What does the picture suggest about the immediate effects of the bomb?

● What do Sawami Katagiri's writings tell you about the immediate effects of the bomb?

When the bomb exploded at Hiroshima, Yurika Hatanake was working behind a concrete shelter 700 metres from the blast. She had a baby with her. She ran to the hills and was caught in the radioactive 'black rain' that fell after the explosion. Her husband takes up the story:

> She found shelter in a shack with some other people and set about feeding the baby. His face was pitted with glass splinters, the largest of which she removed. When the rain stopped, she set out for the hills again. Soon afterwards Yurika's hair started falling out, then she developed small boils and started bleeding from various parts of her body.
>
> By the time I returned home, Yurika was completely bald. The little boy started showing the same symptoms but accompanied by diarrhoea. We managed to contact a doctor but he knew nothing about radioactivity at that time. The boy soon died. Afterwards the doctors believed that the baby on my wife's back acted as a shield, absorbing most of the deadly rays and thus saving her life.

It was clear that this was a completely new type of weapon and a completely new kind of warfare. But there was no turning back. Nuclear weapons had been used. No one could be sure that they would not be used again.

STEP 1

Imagine you are a journalist in 1945. At the end of August, your editor wants you to write an article about the dropping of the atomic bombs on Japan. He insists that your first paragraph must be a short, accurate and powerful summary of this event. Your second paragraph must explain the significance of the event. Your editor wants you to use no more than 40 words in each of your paragraphs.

Rivalry of the 'Superpowers'

The atomic bombs ended the war in 1945, but the world was still not a safe place. There were **new tensions and new fears**. By the end of the war, relations between the **Allies** had gone sour!

- The USA and Britain now saw the Soviet Union as an enemy.
- The Soviet Union saw the USA and Britain as enemies too!

The Americans and the British suspected that the Soviets wanted to take over other countries. They were afraid that the Soviets would soon have their own atomic bombs.

The Soviets were afraid that the atomic bombs used on Japan would now be used on them.

For forty years these two sides spied on each other and threatened each other – but they never actually fought each other. Historians call this the Cold War.

Throughout the Cold War, the USA, the Soviet Union and other countries all worked hard to make nuclear weapons that were more and more powerful.

The race was on to make more and more atomic weapons. This chart shows some of the most important developments in the **Nuclear Arms Race**.

Early events in the Nuclear Arms Race

- 1945 – Atomic bombs dropped on Hiroshima and Nagasaki by USA.
- 1949 – Soviet Union tests its own atomic bomb.
- 1952 – USA tests a hydrogen bomb – hundreds of times more powerful than the bombs dropped on Japan.
- 1953 – Soviet Union tests its own hydrogen bombs.
- 1957 – Britain tests its own hydrogen bomb.
- 1960 – France tests its own atomic bomb.
- 1964 – China tests its own atomic bomb.

There was constant tension in eastern Europe and several **major flashpoints** around the world. War between the West (countries supported by the USA) and the East (countries supported by the Soviet Union) could have broken out in any of these places. This map shows where they were:

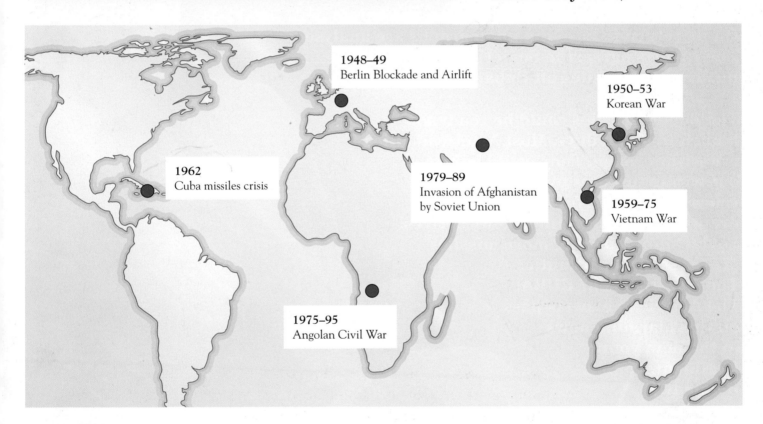

1948–49
Berlin Blockade and Airlift

1950–53
Korean War

1962
Cuba missiles crisis

1979–89
Invasion of Afghanistan by Soviet Union

1959–75
Vietnam War

1975–95
Angolan Civil War

The big question was: would either of the **Superpowers** ever be tempted to use its atomic weapons? Both sides were pushed to the limit in 1962. That was the year of the Cuba missiles crisis, when the world came closest to a full-scale nuclear war.

Think

- Some people say that the world is a safer place with nuclear weapons. Why do you think they say this?

- Some people say that the world is a more dangerous place with nuclear weapons. Why do you think they say this?

The Cuba missiles crisis

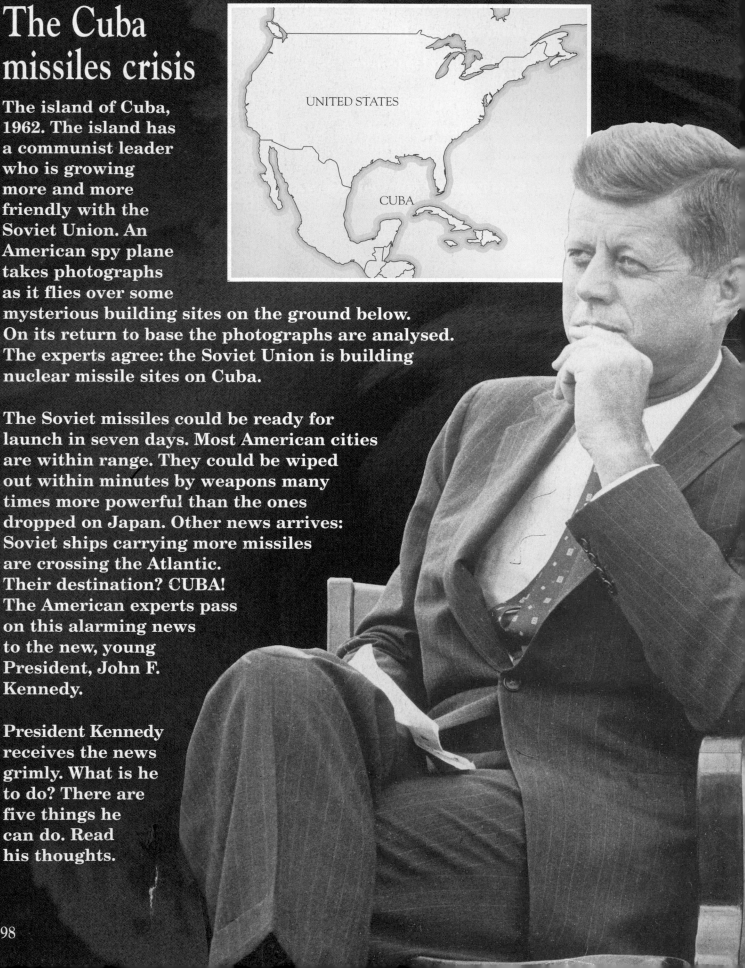

The island of Cuba, 1962. The island has a communist leader who is growing more and more friendly with the Soviet Union. An American spy plane takes photographs as it flies over some mysterious building sites on the ground below. On its return to base the photographs are analysed. The experts agree: the Soviet Union is building nuclear missile sites on Cuba.

The Soviet missiles could be ready for launch in seven days. Most American cities are within range. They could be wiped out within minutes by weapons many times more powerful than the ones dropped on Japan. Other news arrives: Soviet ships carrying more missiles are crossing the Atlantic. Their destination? CUBA! The American experts pass on this alarming news to the new, young President, John F. Kennedy.

President Kennedy receives the news grimly. What is he to do? There are five things he can do. Read his thoughts.

Ask the United Nations to act as a 'go between'?

Invade Cuba?

Stop the Soviet ships from sailing towards Cuba – a 'blockade'?

Do nothing?

Destroy the missile sites by air strike?

Kennedy knows he has to tread a fine line. He does not want to start a nuclear war and yet he does not want to appear weak. The world awaits his decision with baited breath.

Kennedy decides to blockade Cuba. He hopes to buy time so that the USA and the Soviet Union can talk in secret. The Soviet ships stop. The talking begins. But the building of the missile sites continues. The world waits. If the talking fails, a Third World War will follow.

Eventually the leader of the Soviet Union, Khrushchev, says that if the blockade is ended and the threat of an invasion of Cuba is lifted, they will take the missiles off Cuba. The USA agrees. The crisis is over. The USA and the Soviet Union also agree to two things:

- A telephone link is set up between the two leaders, in case another crisis arises.

- A treaty banning the testing of nuclear weapons above the ground is made.

Think

- Look at Kennedy's thought bubbles. Which of these options could have risked a nuclear war?

- Which of these options would make Kennedy seem weak?

Think

- Why might the Cuba missiles crisis have led to a nuclear war?

- Why do you think the Superpowers did not use their nuclear weapons in the end?

STEP 2

Imagine you are a journalist in 1962. Your editor wants you to write an article about the Cuba missiles crisis that has just ended. Your first paragraph should be a short, accurate and powerful summary of the event. Your second paragraph must explain the significance of the event. Use no more than 40 words in each of your paragraphs.

A safer world or continuing danger?

By 1990 communism in the Soviet Union had collapsed. The USA and the Soviet Union stopped being enemies. The threat of a Third World War seemed to go away. But the nuclear danger continued.

Danger 1

In 1962, at the time of the Cuba missiles crisis, the USA and the Soviet Union had 8800 megatons of nuclear weapons between them. By 1990 they had over 20,000 megatons.

A big problem was what the USA and the Soviet Union should do with the nuclear weapons they no longer needed. It is not easy to destroy them. The weapons contain dangerous nuclear material which scientists reckon will take 250,000 years to become safe! So far, no one has found a safe way of getting rid of the material.

They could:

- send it into space ... but what if the rocket carrying it crashed back to earth?

- seal it in underground bunkers or under the sea ... but can anyone guarantee that it will not leak for a quarter of a million years? What if there is an earthquake?

- turn the material into something else ... but no one has invented a reliable way of doing this.

So, for now, nuclear waste is in store. While the stores build up, they are attractive targets for terrorists eager to get hold of their own nuclear weapons.

Danger 2

The old Soviet Union collapsed in 1991. It split into several smaller countries. Many old Soviet nuclear weapons were in these countries. These countries demanded a say about what happened to the weapons. It was impossible for the Russian government to keep a check on where all the weapons went.

Danger 3

Plenty of other countries had managed to build their own nuclear weapons by 1990. Apart from the USA and the Soviet Union, these countries were known to have nuclear weapons:

- Britain
- China
- France
- India
- Pakistan
- Israel
- South Africa.

Many more countries were capable of building nuclear weapons if they had wanted to. Each country wanted nuclear weapons to stop enemies from threatening them.

In order to develop these weapons, nations have carried out nuclear test explosions underground or on remote islands. No one can be sure what damage these tests have done to the environment and to the people who live nearby.

In May 1998 the world was shocked by reports of Pakistan and India testing nuclear weapons. This photograph shows Pakistani children supporting nuclear tests. Since India and Pakistan had secured their **independence** from Britain in 1947 they had been to war with each other three times. News of their weapons-testing led to criticism from western powers.

Think

- Why were other countries alarmed by India and Pakistan's nuclear tests?

- What do you think the governments of India and Pakistan might have thought about the criticism from the rest of the world?

STEP 3

Imagine you are a journalist in 1998. At the end of May, your editor wants you to write an article about the nuclear dangers facing the world. Your first paragraph should be a short, accurate and powerful summary of the situation. Your second paragraph must make a judgement about what is the greatest danger. You have a limit of 40 words for each paragraph.

Thinking your enquiry through

Choose one of the three articles that you have started and design the whole front page of the newspaper. Make sure it has:
- the name of the newspaper
- the date

- a powerful headline
- the two opening paragraphs that you have already written
- further paragraphs to complete your article
- a relevant picture.

101

Death of an empire

How did 'new thinking' destroy the Soviet Union?

In 1917, the **Tsar** of Russia was overthrown by his people. His huge empire fell into the hands of Lenin and his **communist revolutionaries**. Over the next 70 years the communists transformed Russia into a new kind of **empire**. From being a poor and backward land of peasants, it became an enormously powerful **state** known as the Soviet Union. It had a massive army and, by the mid-1980s, it had enough nuclear weapons to demolish the planet. Yet, by 1992, the Soviet Union had collapsed. Statues of Lenin were toppled like the statues of the Tsar at the start of the century. But the Soviet Union was destroyed not by a revolution of the people or by missiles and bombs but by a different kind of power: the power of words and ideas.

The man who unleashed the new ideas that ended the Soviet Union was Mikhail Gorbachev. He was not an enemy of the Soviet Union. He was its leader. When he came to power in 1985, he was worried. He believed that the once-great Soviet Union was in danger of collapse. He was determined to bring it back to life by stirring up what his books and speeches called 'new thinking'. He succeeded in stirring up new ideas – but in doing so he destroyed his own career and the communist state that he was trying to save.

A statue of Lenin on a Russian scrapheap, 1992

Your enquiry

Mikhail Gorbachev changed history by encouraging his people to think differently. In this enquiry you will learn what the communists taught the people of the Soviet Union to believe – and not to believe – for the 70 years before Gorbachev came to power. Finally you will write a diary showing how Gorbachev's new ideas led directly to the collapse of the Soviet empire.

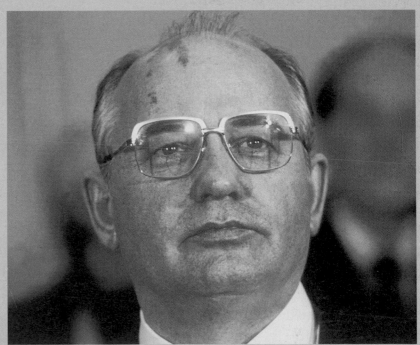

The wealth of the people

Lenin and all other leaders of the Soviet Union were communists. As communists they followed the ideas of a German writer, Karl Marx. Marx died in 1883 but his fame lived on, especially in the Soviet Union, where everyone was taught to believe his ideas about how countries should make and share wealth.

Marx noticed that most countries used a system that he called **capitalism**. In this system people could use money (capital) to start their own business. If the business did well, the owner (or capitalist) could grow rich from the profits. His workers, who really created the wealth, were usually paid low wages. This cartoon shows, in a very simple way, how capitalism works.

Marx believed that capitalism would not last long. He predicted that the workers in each country would rise up in a revolution and take control of the factories and the government. They would then create a system known as **socialism** where people are not allowed to run their own businesses. Instead, the **state** (another word for the government) decides what should be made and sets prices and wages at levels that are fair to the working people. Those same people choose the government, so they are really in charge of the whole system.

Marx thought socialism was much fairer than capitalism. He said that eventually socialism would turn into **communism** where everyone made and shared whatever they needed without any government at all.

Think

- Use the cartoon to describe how capitalism works. (Start with the capitalist.)

- Why did Marx think capitalism was a bad system?

- Why might some people say that capitalism is a good system?

This cartoon sums up socialism in a very simple way:

All through its history, **propaganda** posters like this one taught the people of the Soviet Union to believe that capitalism was an evil system that fed greedy people who created no wealth. Socialism was always shown as the best possible system.

A Soviet anti-capitalist poster, 1931

Think

- Use the cartoon to describe how socialism works. (Start with the people choosing the government.)
- Why did Marx think socialism was a good system?
- Why might some people say that socialism is a bad system?

STEP 1

Look back through pages 104 to 105.

1 Make a list of statements that the leaders of the Soviet Union would want its people to say about how wealth should be made and shared.

2 Make a list of statements that the leaders of the Soviet Union would not want its people to say about how wealth should be made and shared.

The man of steel

Lenin never managed to turn the Soviet Union into a fully socialist state. That task was completed by Lenin's successor, Joseph Stalin. Stalin was not his real name, but he chose to use it because he liked what it said about him. The name meant 'Man of Steel'.

Lenin died in 1924. By 1928 Stalin had taken complete control of the government of the Soviet Union. He was determined to create a massive, powerful and fully communist state. **Nothing would stop him.**

Stalin set about using the power of the state to transform the Soviet Union. The government ran all major businesses. A series of Five Year Plans set targets for all main industries. Production of oil, steel and coal increased massively. Railways and canals were built to link the different industrial areas of the Soviet Union. New cities were built around mines and iron and steel works. At the same time small farms were merged into massive state-owned **collectives** that had to grow exactly what the government ordered.

As early as 1929, Stalin declared that ...

We are leaving behind the age-long Russian backwardness. We are becoming a country of metal, a country of cars, a country of tractors. And when we have put the Russian people in cars and the peasants on tractors, let the capitalists who boast so loudly try to overtake us. We shall see then which countries can be classified as backward and which as advanced.

As you might expect, not everyone agreed with Stalin's socialist approach. In particular, millions of fairly wealthy farmers, known as kulaks, were angry that their land was taken from them and handed over to the state. But it was not wise to resist. Stalin was no ordinary communist. He forced vast numbers of peasants and town labourers who dared to oppose his plans to work as slaves building canals and railways, even during the cruel Russian winters. **Millions died –** but Stalin was convinced that all this suffering was a price worth paying.

One Soviet writer recorded what he saw at this time:

> Trainloads of deported peasants left for the icy north, the forests, the steppes, the deserts. Old folk starved to death in mid-journey, new-born babies were buried on the banks of the roadside and each wilderness had its crop of little crosses of branches or white wood.

Stalin's modernisation of the Soviet Union certainly produced results, despite severe difficulties such as the terrible famine in 1932. This chart shows how industrial output grew between 1928 and 1941. It was an astonishing achievement.

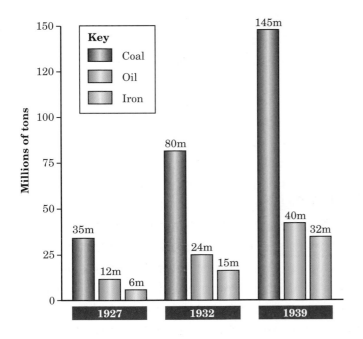

The Soviet Union was catching up on the wealth of capitalist nations such as the USA and Britain, although it concentrated on heavy industry and there was always a severe shortage of consumer goods such as fridges, cookers or even clothing. Soviet citizens were taught to take pride in the growth of industry. No one was supposed to complain that ordinary people got very few of the benefits.

Despite huge set-backs during the Second World War, the Soviet Union continued to build up its industry until about 1960 when production in agriculture and industry began to fall. But Soviet propaganda continued to teach the people that socialism was the path to plenty – even though capitalist countries such as the USA were creating far more wealth.

Think

- From what you have read on these pages, why do you think Stalin liked the name 'Man of Steel'?

STEP 2

Look back through pages 106 and 107.

1 Make a list of statements that the leaders of the Soviet Union would want its people to say about how Soviet industry and agriculture was being developed.

2 Make a list of statements that the leaders of the Soviet Union would not want its people to say about how Soviet industry and agriculture was being developed.

The power of the state

Soviet citizens were taught for many years that their form of government was the only completely democratic system in the world.

A **democracy** is a system of government where the people choose who holds power. In Britain or the USA voters choose between **candidates** from several **parties**. In the Soviet Union, voters chose between candidates from just one party. They could vote any person into power – as long as he or she was a communist.

Soviet voters were taught that there was no need for more than one party because the communists were the party of all people. They were told that even though other countries had more than one party, it was always the rich capitalists who were in control.

The Soviet system was known as a **one-party state**. No opposition to the Communist party was allowed.

Joseph Stalin used this system more violently than any other Soviet leader. He made sure that no one ever challenged his power. Soviet citizens quickly learned that it was dangerous to criticise anything the government did.

No one was safe. Everyone feared the secret police, who would call in the middle of the night and take away anyone who had shown the slightest resistance to Stalin. Communist party leaders, army officers, church leaders, poets and even members of the secret police itself were arrested, tortured, put on trial and sent away to labour camps or shot. Neighbours spied on each other and even children informed on their parents. They were taught that loyalty to the Communist party was more important than anything else.

Think

- What is a one-party state?
- Why might some people say that a one-party state is not a good idea?

This statue was made to remember a 14-year-old Soviet boy, Pavlik Morozov, who informed the secret police that his own father had criticised Stalin. His father was taken away to a work camp – and soon afterwards Pavlik was murdered by members of his own family.

All over the Soviet Union thousands of work camps were built. As many as eight million Soviet citizens were shut away in these brutal camps.

Historians think Stalin ordered the execution of over a million of his own people.

Soviet leaders after Stalin continued his approach but with less brutality. Like Stalin, they used propaganda to highlight the positive achievements of the Soviet Union such as improvements in education, health and the rights of women.

- Soviet books, newspapers, radio, television and films were all censored so that only official communist views were expressed. No British or American films were allowed.
- Schools taught children what to think and discouraged discussion. History lessons followed a text book written by Stalin which showed how all of history had been preparing the world for the success of the Soviet Union.

- Churches were destroyed in many areas. People were told that religion was a poison that stopped people trusting in the Communist party.
- Athletes were given expert training from an early age and often won gold medals at the Olympic Games. The communists could boast that Soviet citizens were the healthiest in the world.
- Soviet scientists managed to put the first man in space in 1961. This was used as a sign that communist technology was outstripping the capitalist West.

Think

- Why do you think Pavlik Morozov was prepared to betray his father?
- Why do you think Stalin even had members of the secret police arrested and punished?

Think

- What different types of communist propaganda can you find between pages 105 and 109?
- Why do you think Soviet people were not allowed to hear radio programmes or watch films from countries such as America or Britain?

In areas on the edge of the Soviet Union, some nationalist groups wanted to break free from Soviet control. But Soviet propaganda said nationalism was foolish and that the whole world would eventually be united in one vast Soviet Union. National differences would fade away.

At the same time as being told how wonderful life was inside their own country, Soviet citizens were told how greedy, violent and corrupt capitalist countries were – and they were told that these western powers were determined to invade and crush the Soviet Union, especially after 1945.

STEP 3

Look back through pages 108, 109 and 110.

1 Make a list of statements that the leaders of the Soviet Union would want its people to say about life in the Soviet Union.

2 Make a list of statements that the leaders of the Soviet Union would not want its people to say about life in the Soviet Union.

Fear of the West

Soviet citizens were taught a long list of examples from history to show how western powers had attacked Russia and the Soviet Union in the past.

Historians are not sure how many Soviet citizens were killed in the Second World War. The figure may be as high as 27 million. This was the sort of figure that was taught in Soviet schools. Britain lost just under half a million people.

Think

- How many more Soviet citizens than British citizens were killed in the Second World War?

- Why do you think the Soviets thought further attacks from capitalist countries in the West were likely?

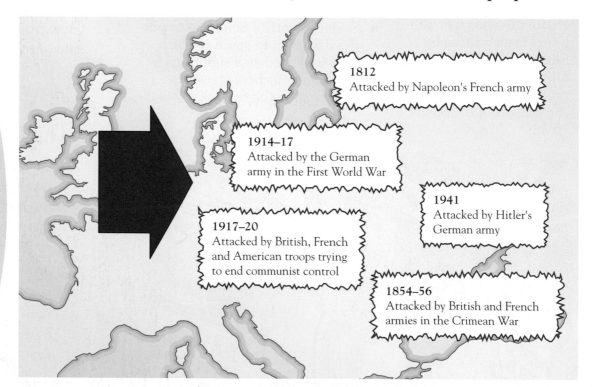

1812
Attacked by Napoleon's French army

1914–17
Attacked by the German army in the First World War

1941
Attacked by Hitler's German army

1917–20
Attacked by British, French and American troops trying to end communist control

1854–56
Attacked by British and French armies in the Crimean War

Western attacks on Russia and the Soviet Union, 1812 to 1945

Soviet leaders promised they would never allow western powers to devastate their land again. As Soviet troops forced Hitler's army back to Germany in 1944 and 1945, the Soviet leaders put communists in charge of states across the whole of eastern Europe. In the Soviet Union people were told that these eastern European countries were delighted to be communist and that they would form a **buffer zone** to protect the Soviet Union from the West.

Western powers accused the Soviets of forcing these countries to turn communist. Winston Churchill, who had led Britain through the Second World War, said that it was as if Europe had been divided by an **Iron Curtain**.

Soviet troops used force on several occasions between 1945 and 1985 to make sure that these eastern European states did not turn away from communism. Soviet leaders such as Khrushchev and then Brezhnev told their citizens that they had to keep communism strong around the Soviet Union. If they did not, the western capitalists would invade as they had done so many times before.

After the USA used its atomic bomb on Japan in 1945, Stalin told his people that the Soviet Union must have its own nuclear weapons to defend itself against attack by the Americans. This was the start of the nuclear **arms race**.

Over the next forty years the USA and the Soviet Union spent enormous sums of money on weapons of all types. The Soviet leaders told their people that if they stopped building new and more powerful arms then their country would be attacked and their whole way of life would be destroyed. (Meanwhile American **presidents** were giving the same message to their own people!)

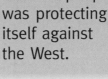

Look back through pages 110 and 111.

1 Make a list of statements that the leaders of the Soviet Union would want its people to say about how it was protecting itself against the West.

2 Make a list of statements that the leaders of the Soviet Union would not want its people to say about how it was protecting itself against the West.

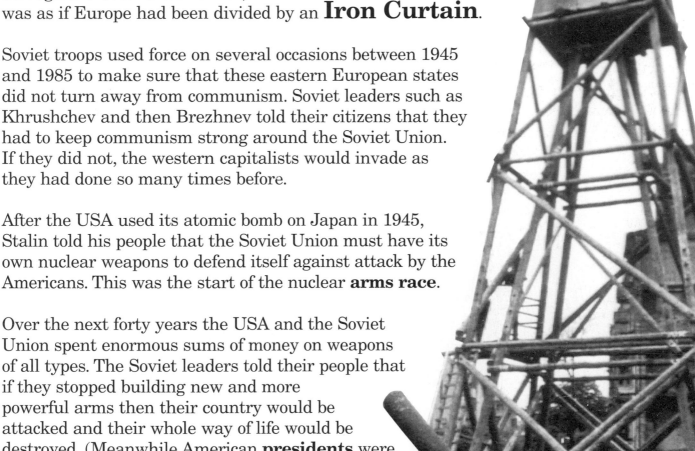

A photograph of a watchtower on the Iron Curtain

Gorbachev's 'new thinking'

You have now seen how the leaders of the Soviet Union kept firm control of their people between 1917 and 1985. In 1985 everything began to change. In that year Mikhail Gorbachev became the new Soviet leader. Like all the leaders since Lenin, Gorbachev was a communist. But he had not risen to power under the influence of Stalin. He believed that the time had come when things had to change.

Gorbachev was convinced that all was not well in the Soviet Union. He made speeches and wrote books to tell people his ideas and to ask them to join in with his 'new thinking'. Here is the cover of an English version of his book. Some of his main ideas are also shown.

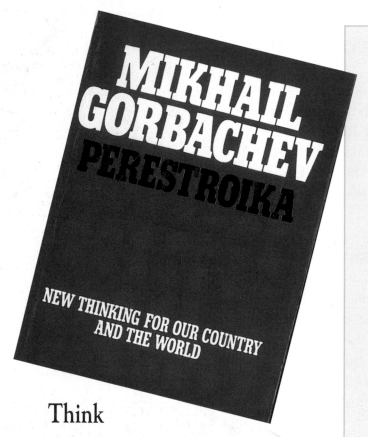

MIKHAIL GORBACHEV PERESTROIKA

NEW THINKING FOR OUR COUNTRY AND THE WORLD

- The Soviet Union is poor. Communism is not creating enough wealth. The economy has been standing still since about 1970.

- The Soviet Union cannot afford to keep up with the Americans' spending on nuclear arms.

- The Soviet Union cannot afford to keep interfering in eastern European countries if they want to turn away from communism.

- We must bring new life and strength to communism in the Soviet Union by letting people have freedom to criticise the way things are done and to suggest improvements.

Think

- Which of these do you think was the Soviet Union's single biggest problem in 1985?

- What might have happened to Gorbachev if he had said things like this when Stalin was still running the Soviet Union?

Over the next six years Gorbachev encouraged Soviet citizens to speak and think with a freedom that they had never known. It had results that Gorbachev had never wanted. This timeline shows what happened.

Gorbachev and the collapse of the Soviet Union

- 1986 – Gorbachev met US President Reagan and told him that he would be cutting back on the Soviet Union's nuclear weapons – even if the USA kept all its missiles.

- 1987 – Gorbachev encouraged freedom of speech and religion. He released many people from camps even though they continued to criticise communism.

- 1988 – Gorbachev announced that he would be greatly reducing Soviet troops guarding eastern Europe.

- 1989 – Gorbachev did nothing when demonstrators ended communism in many eastern European countries. The Berlin Wall was knocked down as a sign that the 'iron curtain' no longer existed.

- 1990 – Gorbachev tried to encourage trade by allowing capitalist businesses to start in the Soviet Union. McDonald's opened a fast food store in Moscow. Gorbachev said non-communist parties would be allowed in the Soviet Union. A popular leader called Boris Yeltsin started a capitalist party.

- 1991 – Some communists tried to remove Gorbachev and to take the country back to Stalin's ways. They failed – but Gorbachev was obviously losing control. Boris Yeltsin was more popular.

- 1992 – The Soviet Union ended on 1 January. It broke up into 15 separate nations. Boris Yeltsin was the leader of the biggest of these – Russia. He promised to follow capitalism not communism. Gorbachev retired from politics!

The death of the Soviet Empire: the communist flag on top of the government headquarters in Moscow is lowered for the last time, 31st December 1991

Thinking your enquiry through

Imagine you are a Soviet citizen. You have been brought up as a strict communist and have always been taught to believe in the greatness of the Soviet Union.

Write a diary entry about each of the events on the timeline on this page. Make sure you always say what you have been taught to believe and why you find Gorbachev's new ideas so shocking. Use the lists you made in Steps 1, 2, 3 and 4 to help you.

Black and British

How should we write the history of black communities in Britain?

It was dark and misty, the brink of daybreak, as the mighty SS Empire Windrush cut through the grey murky river. Timothy Cooper, a young Jamaican, had finally arrived in Great Britain, the Motherland.

He was just one of the hundreds of West Indians jostling for position on board, hoping to steal a glimpse of land over the heads and shoulders. Some of the more eager perched on fragile suitcases, others carefully hoisted their bodies up ropes and poles dotted around the upper deck. Peering through the swarm of passengers, Timothy could just make out the outline of the coast. He was weary from the long journey, but the sight of land lifted his spirit. This was England, the land where he would be judged on his merits. The land where if he worked hard, he would achieve. The land that had so much to offer. The promised land.

From V. Francis 'With Hope in Their Eyes: The Compelling Stories of the Windrush Generation', 1998

Think

● What were Timothy's hopes for life in Britain?

It was June 1948. Timothy was travelling with 491 other Jamaicans on the SS *Empire Windrush*. They were coming to Britain.

The extract is from a book celebrating the 50th anniversary of Britain's first post-war **immigrants** from the Caribbean. It is full of true stories like Timothy's.

For thousands of years, new ethnic groups have helped to change Britain. This has always been so. You know from your history lessons how Romans, Saxons, Vikings and Normans changed the race, culture and language of the people who lived in the British Isles. In modern times this has simply continued. Britain has been influenced by contact with Europeans, Africans and Asians.

There is a mixture of races and cultures in Britain. This makes writing history very tricky. The situation in Birmingham is not the same as that in Bradford, Brixton or Bristol. In London alone, over 160 languages and dialects are now spoken. This is why it is almost impossible to sum up the experience of Britain's **ethnic minorities.** If you, your parents or your grandparents came to Britain from another country you will have your own family stories or community stories. These might be very different from other people's stories.

So how should **historians** tell the story of British ethnic minorities in the second half of the twentieth century? This leads to lots of other questions:

What sort of evidence should we use?

What different types of story are there?

How can we historians find out about these stories?

Should we talk about lots of **stories** or just one **story**?

Your enquiry

You are going to have a go at writing the history of communities in Britain for yourself. You will focus on Afro-Caribbean communities since 1948. You will use three different **themes** or **stories**. In each story you will decide whether the events were **hopeful** or **disturbing**. At the end of the enquiry you will change these stories using your own information and ideas. Then you will be able to write your own, improved history textbook chapters on multi-ethnic Britain.

1 A story of prejudice

In June 1948 the SS *Empire Windrush* docked in Britain. Most of the 492 Jamaicans on board had fought on Britain's side in the Second World War. They were ex-service men.

The press and the cinema newsreels gave them a warm welcome. This is how one newspaper described their arrival:

> What were they thinking of, these 492 Jamaicans, as the Empire Windrush slid upstream between the closing shores of Kent and Essex? Standing by the landing-stage at Tilbury, one of them looked over the unlovely town to the grey-green fields beyond and said, 'If this is England I like it'. A good omen, perhaps. May he and his friends suffer no disappointment.

'Manchester Guardian', 23 June 1948

Think

- Which sentence shows that the writer of this article hoped that the Jamaicans would be happy in Britain?

Some members of the public were not as welcoming as the cameras and the press! In Liverpool, violence broke out as early as August 1948. Mobs of white people attacked the hostels where the West Indians were staying. The new arrivals wondered what the problem was.

This was their 'Mother Country', so why the cold welcome? After all:

- they spoke English
- they shared a love of national sports like football and cricket
- most were very committed Christians
- they had fought on the same side as Britain in the Second World War!

Yet **prejudice** and **racism** soon got worse. In the years that followed there were many stories of terrible violence and **persecution**. In 1958 black communities in North Kensington suffered violence at the hands of young whites. In Middlesborough in August 1961 hundreds of whites went onto the streets chanting racist slogans. These gangs smashed the windows of black families' houses, terrifying the people inside.

It was especially hard to find places to live. West Indians were sometimes greeted by boarding house signs saying, 'NO BLACKS, NO DOGS, NO IRISH'. This photograph from 1953 shows a sign on a door saying, 'NO COLOURED MEN'.

Some low-paid Afro-Caribbeans had to rent rooms in a slum. If they tried to buy or rent homes in better areas, they were abused or attacked. Most therefore stayed in the 'black areas' of London or other big cities, including: Toxteth (Liverpool), St Paul's (Bristol), Butetown (Cardiff), Chapeltown (Leeds), Handsworth (Birmingham), Moss Side (Manchester).

Daily Mirror, 8 September 1958

Think

- How does the article try to persuade the reader that prejudice is wrong? Find as many examples as you can.

This man is Sebert Clarke. He fought for the Commonwealth. Now he's eager to work for the Commonwealth.

Meanwhile many people, black and white, worked hard to **stop** racism. This article was printed in a popular newspaper in 1958:

No. 1: INTRODUCING TO YOU...

They were born in Jamaica. Do you recognise the uniform?

THE BOYS FROM JAMAICA

● People are human beings even though they come in different colours. The main reason for race riots is plain IGNORANCE of this simple truth.

This is the first of a series which Keith Waterhouse is writing to give people the facts about the coloured people. Today — meet the Jamaicans:

Smiling Percival Bennett works on a co-operative farm in Jamaica.

❶ WHERE THEY COME FROM..

HALF the 200,000 coloured people in Britain come from the West Indies, a sunny chain of islands in the Caribbean, between North and South America.

About 70,000 of those are from Surrey, Middlesex and Cornwall—the three counties of Jamaica, British for 300 years.

By the cheapest route, it costs £75 for them to come to Britain—on a British passport.

Jamaicans have been leaving home to look for work since 1884. They helped to build the Panama Canal.

They emigrated to the U.S.A., to Cuba, to South America. After the war, they began to come here.

❷ WHAT THEY DO AT HOME..

JAMAICA makes the sunshine things. Sugar. Bananas. Coffee. Cocoa. Rum. Tobacco.

About half its workers are in these jobs. And about half its produce comes to Britain.

Jamaica exports £49,000,000 of goods a year. Yet unemployment is still one of its big problems.

To keep in world markets, the country that desperately needs to create labour is obliged to import labour-saving machinery from Britain.

Jamaicans come here for jobs—but Jamaica helps to keep Britain in jobs. We make their machinery. And we provide 40 per cent. of their imports.

❸ WHY THEY ARE HERE..

JAMAICA is the big-money island where jobs are few and pay is poor. The £30,000,000 bauxite industry employs fewer than 5,000 people.

The luxury tourist business, earning £10,000,000 a year, has jobs for only 5,700.

One out of every five Jamaican workers is permanently out of a job. And there is big seasonal unemployment among those who do have a job. Pay is as low as this: An unskilled hand in the cigar business earns £2 11s. 6d. for a fifty-three-hour week. A van driver gets £4 15s. A grade one railway fireman gets £5 10s.

Unemployment pay does not exist. The Jamaicans come here for work.

● WHEN WAR CAME...

● During the war, 10,000 Jamaicans came voluntarily to this country to fight for Britain.

● Eight thousand of them went into the Armed Forces, and 2,000 into munitions work.

● ARE THEY WASTERS? In three years, Jamaicans in Britain have sent home £10,000,000 in postal orders to their dependants.

● ARE THEY CRIMINALS? No Jamaican can leave the island without police clearance. Those with criminal records are not allowed to come.

● ARE THEY HEATHENS? Three out of every five Jamaicans are members of a Christian church or group. In Britain, the churches they attend are packed.

● ARE THEY STEALING OUR WOMEN? After the war, all the Jamaicans who came here were men. Nowadays, half of them are wives and children—coming to rejoin their husbands.

● ARE THEY STEALING OUR HOUSES? Many Jamaicans here live in decrepit houses which white people would not take. Some have done renovations themselves.

● ARE THEY STEALING OUR JOBS? Jamaicans today are in steel, coal, Lancashire cotton and public transport. Colour bar or no, there are still few jobs that employers will give to coloured people if they can get white workers instead.

Twenty-two per cent. of the Jamaicans coming to Britain were in white-collar jobs in the West Indies.

But only four per cent. can get office jobs here. Most become transport workers. And that—according to West Indian welfare workers—accounts for the good manners of Jamaican bus conductors.

F A C T S

F A C T S

TOMORROW: Meet the West Africans...

Tackling prejudice

By 1965 it was at last becoming clear to the British government that something needed to be done about race relations. Labour governments passed Race Relations Acts in 1965, 1968 and 1976.

New laws to improve race relations

1968 New Law!

1976 New Law!

It is now **illegal** to encourage racial hatred. A Commission for Racial Equality will be set up.

It has the power to investigate complaints and go to court.

1965 New Law!

Discrimination against black people in public places such as hotels and cinemas is now illegal.

A Race Relations Board will be created.

Despite these laws, problems continued. In 1979 a National Dwelling and Housing Survey made some worrying findings:

- 5% of whites suffered from overcrowded houses
- 20% of West Indians suffered from overcrowded houses.

Overcrowding made it even harder for young people to break down the barriers at school. It was very difficult to invite friends home to listen to music if your whole family lived in one room!

What black youths could do, of course, was to meet on the street. This, too, led to problems. In the 1970s and 1980s groups of young black people meeting on the streets quickly attracted the attention of the police. This was how one black person in Birmingham viewed the problem in 1978:

> There are policemen who are, shall we say, over-eager, over-keen, in carrying out their duties, so that they will pick on black youths for things which we would consider trivial. You cannot be seen talking to your friends for five minutes before a policeman is going to come along and tell you to move on.

Reverend Ermal Kirby (from Handsworth in Birmingham) speaking in an interview in 'Talking Blues', 1978

In the same year, another Christian minister, Pastor Blisset, from Birmingham warned that the frustrations experienced by black people were going to explode:

> The youths in Birmingham are like a time bomb, and sooner or later there is going to be an explosion. I hope to God that the eyes of the government could be opened to this.

Pastor Blisset of the Bethel Church of God Fellowship in Handsworth, 1978

Explosion
Pastor Blisset was right.
'Explosions' soon took place. This is what happened.

In the St Paul's area of Bristol in April 1980 a black cafe owner was arrested. Blacks watching the raid felt that the behaviour of the police was heavy-handed. They were angry. The crowd swelled. Violent rioting soon followed. The rioters injured police officers, destroyed dozens of police cars, looted shops and set cars and buildings on fire.

A year later, in April 1981, violent rioting took place in Brixton. Following this, there were twelve months of similar events in other inner city areas, including Toxteth, Moss Side and Handsworth, and in Wolverhampton, Leicester and Bradford.

The Home Secretary asked Lord Scarman, a senior judge, to find out what happened in Brixton. Lord Scarman said that the riots were the result of years of **discrimination**, disadvantage and neglect. Although he made it plain that the rioters were wrong to be violent, he showed that by 1981 many blacks, especially young blacks born in Britain, saw their situation as **hopeless**.

Lord Scarman made a lot of recommendations. Here are some of them:

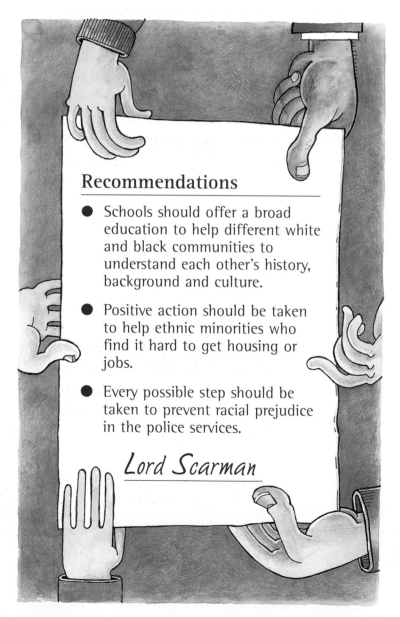

Recommendations

● Schools should offer a broad education to help different white and black communities to understand each other's history, background and culture.

● Positive action should be taken to help ethnic minorities who find it hard to get housing or jobs.

● Every possible step should be taken to prevent racial prejudice in the police services.

Lord Scarman

This helped raise awareness of the problem, but racial prejudice did not go away. A decade later, problems remained. Even in the late 1990s, racial attacks continued, discrimination still existed, prejudice still ruled many minds.

A lot of concern about prejudice still centred on the police. The murder, in 1993, of a black teenager, Stephen Lawrence, led to a big campaign for justice. The Metropolitan Police were accused of failing to carry out a proper investigation. Groups of black people fought hard to show that a terrible injustice had taken place. In February 1999, the MacPherson Report accused the Metropolitan Police of 'institutional racism' in its response to Stephen Lawrence's murder. The government promised a radical change in the laws to combat racism.

STEP 1

Use two small boxes (or two envelopes). Label one 'Hopeful box' and the other 'Disturbing box'. Choose events, developments and examples from sources from pages 116–120. Write them on small red cards and then choose one of the boxes to put them in.

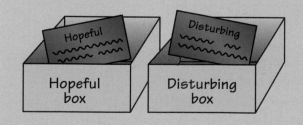

2 A story of changing culture

The story you have just read is only one way of telling the stories of Afro-Caribbean communities in Britain since 1948.

Music, food, art, fashion, entertainment, literature and religion all changed a great deal in the second half of the 20th century. Some of these changes were led by ethnic minority communities.

In the 1960s and 1970s, when a lot of young whites took an interest in eastern religions, some Afro-Caribbeans became interested in the Rastafarian movement. Rastafarianism arose in Jamaica in the 1930s. It had many strands, including African history, African music and stories from the Bible. At the heart of Rasta lay Ethiopia – its history and its future. Rastafarians saw Africa as their spiritual home. Yet what attracted many young people, black and white, was the reggae music of the Rastas.

Whites had long enjoyed many black musical styles – gospel songs, the blues, jazz, ska – all with roots that go back to Africa. But many whites were not aware of the history that gave birth to them. It was the same story with reggae. Teenagers in Britain started to listen to Jamaican music without caring whether they could understand the lyrics.

Many black youths could understand the lyrics quickly. But how could whites understand them unless they knew something of the history that led to them? Gradually young whites began to understand that these songs:

- remembered the days of slavery
- challenged the racism still facing black people
- showed links with Africa.

Reggae music helped to raise awareness of black culture and to change attitudes. Bob Marley, son of a Jamaican woman and a white soldier from Liverpool, was reggae's first superstar. Bob Marley and the Wailers entered the British charts in 1975 and their hits never lost their popularity. Here are some lines from one of their songs:

> Every time I hear the crack of the whip, my blood runs cold.
> I remember on the slave ship, how they brutalized my very soul.

Bob Marley and the Wailers, from the song 'Slave Driver'

Poetry was affected too. This is a picture of Benjamin Zephaniah. In the late 1980s he became Britain's best known Rastafarian poet. This is what another poet said about the effects of Rasta:

> Most Rastas have become so because of the empathy that they have with the music. The movement has brought back to the people a sense of pride in their ancestry.

Jamaican-born Linton Kwesi Johnson, Britain's first popular reggae poet, 1980

Black music did not only help to bring pride in black history. It also changed all kinds of white culture. Many white people started to enjoy black culture without realising it! Soul singer Jazzie B from the band Soul II Soul explained how he felt about this:

When we first started out, I can remember running away from the Teddy Boys who was trying to duff us up, and I can remember a bunch of skinheads and them playing some U-Roy tune, and I'm totally amazed that these guys who try and beat us up were listening to our music!

Soul II Soul's music is a mix of the Euro/colonial, because it really has the whole traces of European pop elements laced with the very essence of roots music, reggae background. I think if you listen to Soul II Soul's music there's no doubt about it, there is always an element of some kind of message or some term of optimism. I think that's like us, and it's to do with our cultural backgrounds as well.

I think we'd be very one dimensional to suggest that Soul II Soul is just a London thing. We are really more of a British thing. I mean, now black Britain has all types of things to be proud of. I'm black and I'm definitely British and that's what I am.

New and old black communities continued to influence the music and fashion of young people. Rap is yet another example of this. Raps became very popular in the 1980s and 1990s with white and black youths. This rap reached the top ten in the British charts in 1983:

I do recall so very well, when I was just a little boy, I used to hurry home from school, I used to always feel, so blue, because there was no mention – in the books we read – about our heritage… And then one day, from someone old, I heard a story never told, of all the kingdoms of my people, and how they fought for freedom, all about the many things we have unto the world contributed…

Gary Byrd, 1983

Think

- How does Gary Byrd's rap help us to understand why it could sometimes be painful to belong to two cultures?

- Compare this rap with Jazzie B's account. What evidence does Jazzie B give us that two cultures were coming together?

Think

- Why was Jazzie B 'totally amazed' at the behaviour of the white youths who tried to beat him up?

STEP 2

Choose events, developments and examples from sources in the section called 'A story of changing culture'. Write them on small yellow cards or pieces of paper. Put them into either the 'Hopeful box' or the 'Disturbing box' that you made in Step 1.

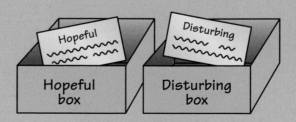

122

3 A story of unequal opportunities?

The problem of jobs

Another way to think about the history of new black communities in Britain is to focus on jobs. Historians need to ask questions about how difficult it was for Afro-Caribbeans to get jobs and how much this changed. Originally, people were encouraged to come to Britain from the West Indies in order to take low-paid jobs. Yet look at this graph showing unemployment figures in 1992!

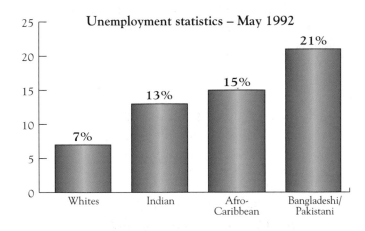

Something had gone badly wrong. What had changed? In the 1970s there was an economic **recession**. From 1973 to 1980 the number of people out of work doubled, but black unemployment went up fourfold. Racism probably played a part in this. One employer asked:

> Why is it wrong for me to refuse to have any of these people in my firm when the government is refusing to have them come into the country?

Quotation from a white employer in 'A Portrait of English Racism' by A. Dummett, 1973

In his report written after the Brixton riots in 1981, Lord Scarman said that one issue in particular led to the tension and violence in the inner city areas – **unemployment**. In Brixton the rate of unemployment among black males under nineteen was 55%. Here is a short extract from his report:

> In a materialistic society, the deprivation caused by unemployment is keenly felt, and idleness gives time for resentment to grow. Many of these difficulties face white as well as black youngsters, but it is clear that they bear very heavily on young blacks who face the burden of discrimination.

From 'The Scarman Report', 1981

Think

- What did Lord Scarman mean by 'the burden of discrimination'?

- Why do you think that he used the word 'materialistic' to describe British society? Why did he think that this made things even worse?

By 1982 one survey found that 60% of Afro-Caribbeans in the 16–20 age-group were without work. In 1983 Leon Brittan, the Home-Secretary said:

> It is a hard fact that ethnic minorities suffer disproportionately from unemployment. There is clear research evidence to back up individual experience of discrimination in recruitment or selection.

It was extra hard for black people to get better-paid office or professional jobs. In 1984 Colin Brown presented his research in a book called *Black and White Britain*. He found that **one in three** white men had a 'white collar' job but only **one in twenty** men of West Indian origin had a 'white collar' job.

To fight the injustice in the workplace, the Commission for Racial Equality came up with a **code of practice**. This came into force in 1984. It had strong support.

Most of the 300 black groups the Commission had consulted

The Confederation of British Industry

Parliament

Attitudes were changing. During the 1980s and 1990s there were efforts to encourage people from different ethnic backgrounds to join the professions. Look at these job adverts.

Think

● What kinds of jobs are these advertisements for?

● What do they tell us about changing attitudes towards ethnic minorities?

● What do they suggest about continuing problems?

124

Choose events, developments and examples from sources in the section called 'A story of unequal opportunities'. Write them on small green cards or pieces of paper. Put them into either the 'Hopeful box' or the 'Disturbing box' that you made in Step 1.

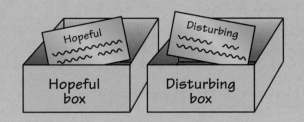

Thinking your enquiry through

It is difficult to write the history of this topic. We, the authors, had many many long discussions about how to write it. We only had a small space in which to tell complicated stories and there are many different views and approaches.

We have used just three types of story. We have concentrated on Afro-Caribbean communities. Now you are going to see what **other ways** you could tell the stories of ethnic minorities since the Second World War.

Story challenge A

As you worked through the three Steps you grouped some of the facts and sources under two headings: 'Hopeful' and 'Disturbing'. Now try to use the points in your 'Hopeful box' to write a 'Hopeful story'.

Then use the points in your 'Disturbing box' to write a 'Disturbing story'. Do some more research so that you can include other important facts and ideas which we have missed out. This might lead to some very different stories!

Story challenge B

This enquiry concentrated on Afro-Caribbean communities. There are many other groups in Britain with different ethnic origins. Do some more research, perhaps drawing upon stories from your own communities. You could try to use the story headings in Story challenge A. You could also try to tell the stories in different ways, using different headings of your own to organise the events and ideas.

When you have finished you will have your own class library of mini-stories on this topic. Write them up in 'little books' and keep them in your boxes!

Rights and wrongs

Can the world live up to its highest hopes?

In 1948, soon after the Second World War, the United Nations Organisation (UNO) set out the Universal Declaration of Human Rights. Some of its main points are shown on this page. Use what you have learned from the enquiries in this book and your knowledge of the world today to discuss the questions.

Think

- Why do you think the UNO produced this Declaration?

- Do you think the Declaration has made any difference to the world?

1 All human beings are born free and equal in dignity and in rights ... and should act towards each other in a spirit of brotherhood.

2 Everyone is entitled to all these rights and freedoms without distinction of any kind, such as race, colour, sex, language, religion, political or other opinion ...

3 Everyone has the right to life, liberty and security of person.

5 No one shall be subject to torture or to cruel, inhuman or degrading treatment or punishment.

7 All are ... entitled to equal protection of the law.

8 Everyone has the right to an effective remedy for acts violating [these] rights.

9 No one shall be subjected to arbitrary arrest, detention or exile.

11 Everyone is to be presumed innocent until proved guilty ...

17 Everyone has the right to freedom of thought, conscience and religion.

18 Everyone has the right to freedom of opinion and expression ...

21 Everyone has the right to take part in the government of his country ... The will of the people shall be the basis of the authority of government; this will shall be expressed in genuine elections by secret vote ...

26 Everyone has the right to education. Education shall be free, at least in the elementary and fundamental stages. Elementary education shall be compulsory ... education shall be directed to the full development of the human personality and to the strengthening of respect of human rights and fundamental freedoms. It shall promote understanding, tolerance and friendship among all nations, racial or religious groups ...

28 Everyone has the right to a social and international order in which the rights and freedoms set forth in this declaration can be fully realised.

29 Everyone has duties to the community. In the exercise of his rights and freedoms, everyone shall be subject only to such limitations as are determined by law for securing ... the rights and freedoms of others ... and the general welfare in a democratic society.

Glossary

abdication — When a ruler such as an emperor chooses to give up all power

alliance — An agreement or partnership between countries, e.g. to help to defend each other's land

allies — Partners, members of an alliance

Allies — The name given to Britain, France, the Soviet Union and the USA in the Second World War

anti-Semitism — Hatred of Jews

appeasement — Avoiding conflict by giving someone most of what he or she demands

aristocrats — Nobles

arms race — Competition between countries trying to have the most powerful armed forces

artillery — Heavy guns, cannon

assassinate — To murder a leader, such as an emperor

Axis powers — The name given to the alliance of Germany and Italy in the Second World War

blockade — Preventing supplies from reaching a place

Bolsheviks — Russian communists

buffer — Something which absorbs the impact of an attack

candidate — A person who asks voters to elect him into power

capitalism — A system where individuals are encouraged to use their talent and money to run businesses that make themselves and their country richer

civilians — Ordinary members of the public, not soldiers

code of practice — An agreement to behave by certain high standards

collective — Large-scale workplace, e.g. Soviet farms

colonies — Lands taken and ruled by another country

communism — A system where all property is shared fairly between people

communist — Someone who believes in communism

concentration camp — Place where a government keeps its opponents prisoner

conscription — Making people join the armed forces

currency — Money

democracy — A system of government where people vote to choose their leaders

dictator — A leader who has complete power

diplomat — Adviser

discrimination — Failing to treat people equally

economic depression — A collapse in trade causing great unemployment

empire — A group of countries ruled by one person, the emperor

ethnic minorities — Groups of people who belong to a race that is different from most other people in that country

evacuation — Taking people away from a danger area

extermination — Mass murder

genocide	Murdering a whole race or nation	**Prime Minister**	The leading politician in a government
heir	The person who is to take the throne on the death of the monarch	**propaganda**	Spreading misleading information to control what people believe
Holocaust	A name given to the mass murder of 6 million Jews	**racism**	Treating people badly or differently because they belong to a different race
Home Rule	The right of a country such as Ireland to have its own Parliament while still being part of the British Empire	**reparations**	Payments made to cover damage caused by war
immigrants	People who move into a country to live there	**republic**	A country which has no monarch
imperial	To do with an empire	**revolution**	Overthrowing a government by force or making any great change
independence	Being free from the control of another power or nation	**self determination**	The right of people to have the freedom to run their own country
interpretation	A version of something that puts across a particular point of view	**Sinn Fein**	An extreme Irish republican party
isolationism	The USA's plan to keep out of any problems in Europe after the First World War	**socialism**	A system where the government controls how wealth is created and shared, and private businesses are not allowed
nationalist	Someone with a fierce pride in their own homeland who wants it to be free to rule itself	**state**	A nation or its government
Nazi	The political party run by Adolf Hitler in Germany	**superpowers**	Countries with massive wealth and/or armed forces
one-party state	A country where only one political party is allowed	**synagogues**	A Jewish place of worship
party	A group of people who share the same ideas about how to run a country	**terrorists**	People who use violence to get what they want from a government
persecution	Picking on or attacking another person or group	**treaty**	Written agreement between nations
policy	A plan of action	**tsar**	Emperor of Russia
prejudice	Judging people or ideas unfairly without considering the facts	**Unionist**	Someone who wants Ireland to remain part of the United Kingdom, usually a Protestant
President	The head of a republic		